T0067436

<u>What Others Are Saying About *Journey to Bliss*</u>

This is a book filled with vision, passion, and heart. Larry Pearlman has succeeded in extracting and magnifying what's really important in life. After reading these inspiring ideas, you will want to get up and do something to make your journey the highest and brightest expression of your spirit. Well done, Larry!

—Alan Cohen, author of A Deep Breath of Life

This book is a rare glimpse at the journey we all must take into the light. The insights illuminate the path of spiritual awakening, and in a simple, clear way show us that we're all making the journey together. If you're looking for a book that will show you the steps you must take to awaken to your Divine Purpose, this is it.

—James Twyman, NY Times Bestselling Author of The Moses Code and Emissary of Light

It's no wonder the thirteen people you'll meet in *Journey to Bliss* chose Larry Pearlman to scribe their *regular-people-find-their-inner-extraordinary* stories, because Larry's a bliss-finder as well. Okay, he might argue about who chose whom, but I believe people who live real lives usually find their tribe, too. Here Larry introduces us to more members of his, and this book is a collection of their fascinating true tales.

Finding the way home is a leitmotif threaded through these diverse accounts. Like I did, I think you'll find the characters' perseverance and the authenticity of their stories inspiring, as you sense their indomitable spirits.

—John Clinton Gray, author of *Gift of Seeds* and *If I Die Thursday*

Larry Pearlman has written an easy to read, stimulating book. It shows us how a variety of good people found and fulfilled their own bliss by listening and responsibly answering a deep inner call to help others.

—Jon Mundy, Ph.D., author of *Living A Course in Miracles.*

JOURNEY TO BLISS

Stories to Inspire You to Find and Follow Your Passion

L A R R Y   P E A R L M A N

BALBOA.
PRESS

A DIVISION OF HAY HOUSE

Balboa Press books may be ordered through booksellers or by contacting:

Balboa Press
A Division of Hay House
1663 Liberty Drive
Bloomington, IN 47403
www.balboapress.com
1 (877) 407-4847

Because of the dynamic nature of the Internet, any web addresses or links contained in this book may have changed since publication and may no longer be valid. The views expressed in this work are solely those of the author and do not necessarily reflect the views of the publisher, and the publisher hereby disclaims any responsibility for them.

The author of this book does not dispense medical advice or prescribe the use of any technique as a form of treatment for physical, emotional, or medical problems without the advice of a physician, either directly or indirectly. The intent of the author is only to offer information of a general nature to help you in your quest for emotional and spiritual well-being. In the event you use any of the information in this book for yourself, which is your constitutional right, the author and the publisher assume no responsibility for your actions.

Any people depicted in stock imagery provided by Thinkstock are models, and such images are being used for illustrative purposes only. Certain stock imagery © Thinkstock.

Print information available on the last page.

ISBN: 978-1-5043-6029-6 (sc)
ISBN: 978-1-5043-6030-2 (e)

Balboa Press rev. date: 08/22/2016

CONTENTS

About The Author vii

Other Books By Larry Pearlman ix

Dedication xi

Acknowledgements xiii

Preface xv

Introduction xvii

The Amazing Story After Love at First Sight 1

The Miracle Worker of Ghana 13

Little Gourmet Son 29

Finden Himmel 45

Creating The Garden 63

Called By Love 79

The White Lion Lady of Timbavati 89

The Changing Face of Bliss 103

The Ugly Sweater 125

Led By the Hand of God 137

Telling Stories 147

The Banker Turned Photographer 163

Houses of Healing 173

Epilogue 187

ABOUT THE AUTHOR

Larry Pearlman experienced his own journey to bliss - twice. The first time was about vocation. The story of how a telephone pole determined his life's work is recounted in the second chapter of his first book, *Journaling The Journey: 25 Spiritual Insights to Light The Way*. That encounter led to a 32-year career as an award-winning salesman, sales manager, and sales trainer in corporate America. It also led him to start his own company, "Creative Expressions Unlimited", through which he offers public talks and workshops. More important, it revealed to Larry that being a salesman, and later a speaker and trainer, was the right path for him to find and follow his bliss.

The odyssey described in *Journaling The Journey* also led him to recognize and follow a second path — one that led him to spiritual bliss. This path brought him into contact with several spiritual teachers and a fuller knowledge of the truth of himself. Interestingly, he discovered that these two paths were not separate but rather overlapping. Ultimately, he found that he could experience and express his passion for life through virtually anything. It was not, in fact, *what* he was doing that brought him bliss. The passion for life, another name for bliss, was already inside of him. He was bringing it *to* whatever he was doing.

In addition to his corporate career, Larry taught courses in "The Art of Creative Living" and served as a faculty member for "The Opening" - an

8-day experiential class in discovering your full potential. For two years, Larry hosted the radio show, "Evolution in Consciousness," interviewing leaders in the "new consciousness" movement like Barbara Marx Hubbard, Gregg Braden, James Twyman, Lynne McTaggart, Joan Borysenko, and Matthew Fox. At 60 years old, he served in the Peace Corps in Ghana for 27 months and then spent three years living at Sunrise Ranch, an intentional, spiritual community in Loveland, Colorado.

He is currently an author and public speaker and offers workshops on "Finding and Following Your Bliss." In addition, he co-facilitates nine-day Costa Rica Retreats with his partner, Susannah Light through her company Divine Nature Tours. For more information about Larry, please visit his website at www.LarryPearlman.com.

OTHER BOOKS BY LARRY PEARLMAN

As a literary person, I had a hard time with the common but, in this case, inaccurate title of this page. It should read "Other Book By Larry Pearlman." I kept it as is because I believe in manifesting reality in advance. In any case, here it is:

Journaling The Journey: 25 Spiritual Insights to Light The Way

DEDICATION

This book is dedicated to Deborah Couch and Wayne Dyer.

I'm guessing that you have heard of Wayne Dyer. In following his bliss unerringly, Wayne brought bliss to literally millions of people. From his book, *I Can See Clearly Now*, I'd like to have Wayne speak to each reader of this book with these words:

"For decades now I've encouraged everyone to believe that making a good living at what you love is a possibility. If you stay on purpose and are committed to following your bliss, the universal one mind will cooperate with you in bringing this to fruition. The right people will show up, the obstacles will be swept away, the necessary circumstances will materialize and guidance will be there."

"Never forget that you are one of a kind. Never forget that if there weren't any need for you in all your uniqueness to be on this earth, you wouldn't be here in the first place."

I'm also guessing that you have not heard of Deborah Couch. Deb did not inspire millions of people. She did not write a book, play great music, have her art hung in the Louvre, or leave poetry behind to touch the hearts of future generations. She simply lived a kind, loving life. In doing so, she inspired most people who knew her; and, because of that, she lives on in our hearts. Deb had just discovered her vocational passion — helping people as a health coach — when cancer took her, but she had always expressed her bliss in everyday life with her smile, her compassion, her humor, and her kindness. She also found bliss with her partner, Phyllis, whom she loved deeply. We miss you Deb.

ACKNOWLEDGEMENTS

This book would not exist if not for the people who agreed to let me tell their stories. I so enjoyed taking a peek into the lives of these wonderful and most interesting people. My appreciation, respect, and love are, therefore, extended fully to Linda Tucker, Dr. David Mensah, Susannah Light, Colin Mead, Edward Bixby, Pris, Andrew Horwood, Andrew Bacon, Leon Keenan, Gary Winkler, Maureen VanHoek, Anne Fuchs and Alicia Sully. I consider you all my friends now, and I hope you make lots more friends from the people who read your stories.

I would also like to mention a few people who gave me the pleasure of listening to their stories even though they are not a part of this book. There were different reasons for that, and those stories may show up in a future book. For now, thank you Chris Marchetti, Maya Kollman, Barbara Bingham and Ben Sigman for allowing me to get to know you better.

As in ALL of my previous books (that would be one), I owe a great debt (and I'd be broke if they asked for their value in money) to my amazing sister, Carol Winkler, and my best friend, Phyllis Warren. Carol was again my editor for this book; and this time, Phyllis joined the editing team. Without them, zillions of commas would be in the wrong place, and you would be wondering how anybody could write such long sentences without taking a breath. Far more than that, however, they were kind enough to let me know when my writing was unclear, wandering, or just plain bad. People who love you can do that. Thanks to both of you many times over. I seriously think that Carol put more time into this book than I did!

The phrase "self-published book" is an outright lie. Though I am technically the publisher of this book, it would never have seen the light of day, much less the warmth of your hands, if it hadn't been for Balboa Press.

I would also like to thank John Deven for helping me with the photographs. The originals were sent to me by each of the subjects of this book and I found out that many of them did not meet Balboa's requirements for resolution quality. John resampled all the images for me, which was a huge help since I don't even know what that means, much less how to do it! Check out www.JohnDevenPhotography.com to see the amazing work he does with his own camera.

PREFACE

Take a group of at least 30 people, pick any 10 at random, and you could write a book about their stories. That's my belief based on fascinating stories I've heard everywhere I go. So, here is that book, although I decided against the random part. I'm sure that would work; however, I'll save that for another book. Instead, I chose to key in on a particular type of story.

In my first book, *Journaling The Journey: 25 Spiritual Insights to Light The Way,* I included the story of how a telephone pole helped me find my bliss. In this book, I want to go beyond that one example to inspire other "ordinary" people, like you and me, to find the path that leads to what makes life fulfilling for them. Beyond that, I want to encourage you to follow that path. I would also like to make it clear that there are all kinds of ways to find your bliss. You don't need a telephone pole or a grand plan of some kind, although that is one way to get there.

We have all read amazing stories of famous people who have overcome great odds to find their bliss and, along with it, fame and fortune. Though inspirational to some, many may see these people as "special" –- people who would have found their way to great heights no matter what their circumstances. In this light, the readers of the story may not truly find inspiration, because they don't feel that they are that kind of "special" person. They are not, therefore, moved to make changes in their own life. Recognizing this, I have chosen to tell the stories of non-famous people, everyday men and women, to eliminate the "I'm-not-that-kind-of-person" excuse.

I have broached the boundary of what could be considered "famous" with two of my subjects, Linda Tucker and Dr. David Mensah. Linda is well known in the conservation world and has written two outstanding books. David is well known in northern Ghana and has written a book documenting his amazing path through life. However, because the average person on the street has probably never heard of them, they fit my definition of "non-famous." Besides, their stories are so compelling that I couldn't resist putting them in the book. Both Linda and David deserve to be famous for what they are doing. At least now, YOU will know who they are.

Perhaps by reading their stories, plus the other eleven in this book, you will be inspired to discover *your* story and share *your* gift with the world.

If you are already living your bliss, and have an interesting story, contact me at <u>larry.pearlman@yahoo.com</u> and tell me about it. Maybe you can be in my next book!

Author's Note

The introductions to each story are told in first person from my point of view. For no reason other than it felt right to me, some of the stories in this book are told in third person and some of them are told in first person. The latter are denoted by "As told by…" just under the title. I hope this note will keep it from being confusing for the reader.

With their permission, I have used the actual names of the subjects of these stories but, in many cases, the names of people mentioned within them have been changed.

INTRODUCTION

"There is a vitality, a life force, an energy, a quickening that is translated through you into action, and because there is only one of you in all of time, this expression is unique. And if you block it, it will never exist through any other medium and it will be lost. The world will not have it. It is not your business to determine how good it is nor how valuable nor how it compares with other expressions. It is your business to keep it yours clearly and directly, to keep the channel open."
Martha Graham - 20th century dancer, choreographer and founder of the Martha Graham Dance Company.

Most of us have heard the expression, "follow your bliss," so let's start out by defining "your bliss."

Your bliss is that thing that you do that lights you up. Time stands still while you're doing it. Joy pours forth from you. You feel like this is what you were born to do. As Wayne Dyer puts it, "Your passion is what stirs your soul and makes you feel like you're totally in harmony with why you showed up here in the first place." Interestingly, as you'll see in the stories of the people in this book, that can take on a wide variety of appearances. It might show up for you in the form of lumberjacking, dancing, farming, teaching, making clothes, building furniture, flower-arranging, racing, or, in my case, being a professional salesman. There is no end to what bliss might look like, so don't put any limitations on what it might be for you. Simply see what *feels* right when you're doing it.

The above Martha Graham quote is as good a way as any to describe what your bliss is. She also touches on *why* you should do it. You are the *only* chance that the world has to experience what was meant to come through you. Jesus, Moses, Mother Theresa, Gandhi, and Albert Schweitzer have one thing in common. They were among the most Selfish people in the world. Why do I say that? Because all of them did only what brought them the greatest satisfaction. That is what your bliss is. It is that which brings you fulfillment in life. This is what might be called "Divine Selfishness". When the word "selfish" is spelled with a small "s," it describes the behavior of someone acting out of their human ego state trying to *get* what they think will make them happy. This never works. If you've tried it, then you know what I mean. When spelled "Selfish," it describes the behavior of people, like those mentioned above, who allow the Truth of themselves to blossom into full expression — bringing their maximum Self into the world. These are people who are *giving* what they deeply feel is truly theirs to give. This is what it means to follow your bliss.

In this book, I'll introduce you to thirteen people who have found their bliss. Among them, you will meet a hair dresser, an opera singer, a restaurant owner and the founder of a spiritual community in Costa Rica. You'll get to know a woman who gave up the glamorous life of modeling to take on the challenging, dangerous, and low-paying task of saving an endangered species. The diversity is to show you that nobody can define your bliss but you.

This book celebrates the journey, and getting there isn't always easy, as some of these stories will show. You'll read about a very rocky road in the case of an orphan growing up in a small African village. You'll be amazed by what he did with his life. In the end, it's always worth the struggle. Sometimes, there is no struggle, but rather an easy, natural outworking. Such was the experience of a construction company owner who is now operating a green cemetery and championing this non-mainstream approach across the country.

I hope you have as much fun getting to know these folks as I had. More than that, I hope that you're inspired to find YOUR bliss and follow it.

Bronnie Ware was a hospice nurse who interviewed more than 800 dying people. In her book *The Top Five Regrets of the Dying*, she lists the number one regret as, "I wish I had had the courage to live the life that I knew I was destined to live." Don't let this be your greatest regret.

Simply find your passion and live it. When you do, you will make a difference in the world.

INTRODUCTION TO "THE AMAZING STORY AFTER LOVE AT FIRST SIGHT"

Maybe you're one of those people who married the boy next door who used to walk you to school every day starting in the third grade. Maybe you married the Vice-President of Marketing that you got to know really well while working on all of those creative projects together. Perhaps Great Expectations, Match.com, or another computer dating service was the road to your soul mate. Or a blind date set up by a college roommate. It might have even been an ambush set by your Aunt Rose when she invited you for dinner and "that cute boy from synagogue" just happened to be there that night.

There are lots of "how-I-met-my-spouse" stories out there, and I love to hear them. I've heard a lot of them. Only once have I heard a story that took place over a seven year period between that first magic moment of knowing he was the one to the first word being spoken. Meet Maureen VanHoek...............

THE AMAZING STORY AFTER LOVE AT FIRST SIGHT

as told by Maureen VanHoek

I knew that Jan was the man I would marry when I first saw him. Even better, he was equally drawn to me. Recipe for a whirlwind romance, engagement and marriage, right? Well, would you believe that it was seven years from that first sighting to when I spoke my first word to him? Why? Well, let's go back to that first sighting, which was pretty amazing in itself.

I was 23 years old and working as a secretary in the Boston office of a national company. In March of 1993, my boss asked me to go down to Orlando, Florida, to work with the staff there preparing for the company's annual customer conference. Nothing too exciting — simply be a go-fer, helping wherever I was needed. We went down a day early, and I was talking to my boss out by the pool. Jan was a hot-shot sales director in our Chicago office and was hanging out with all the pretty-boy sales people on the other side of the pool. When I first saw him, I gasped. Never in any dream or fantasy had I ever seen a man this handsome, this striking, this.......perfect. I **knew** that I would one day marry him.

But on **that** day, I didn't even have the courage to say hello to him! Now, I have always been able to talk with anyone, but words refused to come out of my mouth when he was near me for the rest of that week. I went about my business, stealing glances at him when I could, absolutely sure that everyone in the room must be hearing the pounding of my heart. If I saw him walking my way, I'd find a place to hide. Somehow, I managed to do my work during the rest of the conference. I'm not sure how I did anything correctly since my mind was filled with nothing but thoughts of him. What I didn't know was that he felt the same way about me!

<u>Second Year</u>

Fast-forward a year to the time of the next annual conference. We had never spoken a word to each other during that first conference; nor had we any occasion to be in contact since — though I had thought of him sooooo many times. Sure enough, I was asked to go down to Orlando again in the same role. My co-workers must have wondered why my excitement level was so high about simply helping to set up the conference.

Sure enough, Jan was there again. I may have been a year older but my courage hadn't grown any. I still could not talk to him, even though there were many times I could easily have walked up to him and found some excuse to engage in conversation. On the second day of the conference, I felt a tap on my shoulder. I turned to see Jan standing in front of me with a big smile on his face. "Hi, I'm Jan VanHoek. I saw you at last year's conference and wanted to meet you. What's your name?" Now most people would consider that a simple question and an easy, comfortable way to finally have the meeting for which I had been yearning. But again I froze. Have you ever seen the old Abbot and Costello movies where Costello sees Frankenstein (not that Jan reminded me of Frankenstein!) and is so scared that his mouth opens but nothing comes out? That was me. Even when Jan made a couple more comments and asked another question I couldn't utter a word. I just stood there, mortified, staring at him with my brain disengaged. After about an hour (probably 60 seconds, but to me it felt like an hour), he said something about maybe seeing me later. Then he walked away. How was I ever going to marry this man if I couldn't even speak to him? Still, in my heart I knew it was to be. I returned to Boston at the end of the conference without going beyond that first awkward meeting.

Third Year

Now I've been told that I'm an attractive woman. It wasn't like I had no opportunities to date, but my heart only had room for Jan. Even though I still had not met or even spoken a single word to him, I had not dated at all since the first day I laid eyes on him.

History repeated itself in the third year as I was again chosen to attend the conference in Tampa, as was Jan. By this time, I had made a name for myself with the international crew and was well known by the conference participants. I was in the conference booth registering all of the attendees when I saw Jan coming toward me. I panicked and hid under the booth! The person I was working with thought I was crazy. I just shushed her and told her to ignore me. When I heard his voice, I was so startled that I picked my head up and hit the table. I held my breath, hoping he would not look under the table. It just wouldn't do to have my future husband meet me while I was hiding under a table! It felt like I didn't take another breath until he had walked away. Again, I let the whole week go by without ever speaking to him.

Fourth Year

You know the script by now, but this year it got more interesting, and humiliating from my point of view. The conference was now being held in San Diego. Again, he filled my thoughts during the whole week without a single word being spoken between us. This time, however, I had a little help in keeping us apart, as if I needed any.

Though I had gone out of my way to avoid Jan the past three years, I had gotten to know most of the people on the teams that had been set up for the conferences. A group of girls had learned about my infatuation with Jan, and one of them was rather obsessed with him herself. She spent the entire conference doing her best to keep us from meeting. I, therefore, returned to Boston once again without having been introduced to Mr. Right.

Fate Brings Us Together

Believe it or not, this went on for seven years! The final conference was in March of 1999. By that time, I had been promoted to Marketing Manager in Boston, and Jan had recently become Vice President of Sales in the Chicago office. The VP of Marketing came to my desk one day with an assignment. "There's a rising star in the Chicago office named Jan VanHoek. I want you to go out there and work with him on putting together a new product brief for a software product he is selling. I need this immediately. Here's your plane ticket for tomorrow."

With my heart in my throat, I composed myself, called Jan, introduced myself and requested the meeting. "Can't do it tomorrow, Maureen. I've got meetings backed up all day." When I insisted that I was under a deadline, he said that I could come out and we could begin working on it over dinner after the work day. The phone rattled from the shaking of my hand as I hung up. I was finally going to take the first step to meeting my groom.

An hour later, that same phone rang. After confirming that I was coming out to meet with Jan the next day, the woman on the other end said, "Watch your back, honey. Jan asked me to get something from his desk. I saw a picture of you in a red dress in his top right-hand drawer. Maybe he has some kind of a thing for you." I can't even remember the rest of that conversation. A red dress! The only time I had ever worn a red dress where he could have taken a picture was at the very first conference. I couldn't have had a clearer sign that we were meant for each other.

The Beginning

I brought two suitcases on that trip — BIG suitcases — for ONE night! I was going out to work on a product brief, but we were going to dinner. Was this a date or a business meeting? What kind of restaurant were we going to? Couldn't chance not having the perfect clothes. When I got to Chicago, I had two friends come over to my hotel room. I tried on outfit after outfit, changing my mind over and over again.

I didn't want to send the wrong message, so I chose a smart business-oriented ensemble. When I saw how nervous he was as I walked into his office I realized that this was a date! I couldn't go on our first date in business clothes! You should have seen how confused he looked when I told him to wait for me while I went back to the hotel to change.

If I had any doubt that this was a date, it vanished when he took me to Vivo — a high-end, very romantic, Chicago restaurant. I had never been to a fancy restaurant before. I was a small-town girl who was blown away by this beautiful, expensive, plush place. It was obvious that this was nothing new to him. As soon as we were seated, what were the first words I spoke to this man that I was so passionate about? "I am not one of those girls. If you're here for sex, think again!" He smiled and said, "OK, thank you." Not letting it drop, I waited just a few minutes before saying, "No, I want to be very clear. I am not going to be another notch on your bedpost." This time he replied, "Maureen, thanks for your clarity. Why don't we do this: when I ask, you can tell me 'no', but I haven't asked."

This was the last week of November, 1999. I was twenty-nine years old and having my first glass of wine. At the end of dinner, he invited me to come over for a cup of coffee. I said, "Absolutely not." When he insisted that he was just asking me to have a cup of coffee at his place, I told him that I didn't drink coffee and could he please call me a taxi. Being a gentleman, he did just that. Being a man, he asked, as I got into the taxi, "Are you sure?" I was, and I think that made him want me that much more.

Two weeks later, I flew out again for another business meeting. The day I was flying out, a car sideswiped me and totaled my week-old, gorgeous, black, convertible Mitsubishi Eclipse for which I had worked so hard. If it weren't for Jan, I would have canceled my trip, but I **really** wanted to see him again. I had my uncle drive me to the airport. By the time I landed, I had a bad case of the flu coming on. I mentioned it to Jan when I called him to confirm that I had landed. He showed up with Nyquil packaged up in a bow and a box of Issey Miyake perfume. I dabbed on the perfume and couldn't believe how beautiful it was. It was perfect for me. I've never worn another perfume since that day, and I still have the box from that first bottle!

During that trip, he told me that he had made a commitment to a female "friend" to spend New Year's Eve with him. He wanted me to know about it, even though she was only a friend. Not only did I tell him that it was fine, but I made up a huge, beautiful gift basket for him when I got home. It included champagne, two champagne glasses, and cheese and crackers. I sent it to him with a note telling him that I hoped the two of them had a wonderful New Year's Eve.

The most romantic man in the world called me on December 30 and told me he had cancelled his "friend's" visit because he knew it wasn't right. He didn't want to jeopardize what we had. He waited for me to come out on January 2, and we celebrated the beginning of the magical year 2000 with the champagne I had sent him. I still have those glasses!

Three months later, I turned down an interview with the executive producer of ABC Action News for what I had thought was my dream job. Instead, I accepted Jan's invitation to move to Chicago and live with him. I thought it was a bit strange that every day Jan would ask me, "Are you feeling lucky today?" Every day, for five days of fruitless job hunting I'd tell him, "No - not really." On the sixth day, I landed a job interview, and when he asked me that same question again, I exclaimed, "YES - I feel really lucky today!" He then said that we should go out to eat that night, but he had to have his lucky black shirt. For some reason, he had trouble finding it but ignored my suggestion that he could just wear another shirt. He insisted that he had to have his lucky shirt that night and was so relieved when he found it. He was really nervous when we got to the restaurant, and then he handed me this box. I said, "Oh, Jan — you don't have to give me gifts. I am just so happy to be with you." He suggested that I might really want to look at this one, but I insisted that I didn't want any gift. When he persisted, I told him I would only open it if it was something we could share, to which he replied, "Absolutely."

Okay, you all know exactly what was in that box, but I really didn't get it. I was hoping for chocolate! Just so you don't think I was totally brainless, you have to understand that this was a pretty big box. Of course, it contained another box which contained another box. That third box was a stunning mahogany and oak box. Believe it or not, I was so taken with the beauty of that box that I still didn't get it until I opened it and saw the ring. I was stunned. I put the box on the table and heard him say, "Well?" After a long pause, I could only manage to stammer out some meaningless noises. I then had the only out-of-body experience I have ever had as I saw myself sitting there. Then I realized that there was not a sound in the restaurant. Everybody was watching and waiting for my answer. My nervousness built to a crescendo and when he said, "So?," I started laughing. Then I started crying. Then I said, "You have to ask." He did, and when I said, "Yes," the whole restaurant exploded into applause. We were married in Newton, Massachusetts on November 7, 2001.

So that was my journey to bliss. I have much in my life that I love — my two children, my work, my friends; but I can honestly say that it is my relationship with Jan that is the center of it all.

PostScript

I first heard Maureen's story in 2002. I often ask couples how they met and this was the best story I had ever heard. I repeated it often and when I decided to write this book, I knew I had to include her story. Tracked her down using social media (of course), and I am so glad that I did. "The rest of the story," as Paul Harvey used to say, is even more incredible.

Maureen and Jan have been happily married for fourteen years now, and people in their neighborhood think of them as the perfect "Barbie and Ken" couple. Why wouldn't they? They are two stunningly attractive people who still adore each other. They live in a beautiful home. Each has a high-income job that they love. They have two beautiful sons. Anybody would love to be in their shoes, right? Well, maybe. But how many people would jump at the chance after learning that Lucas, nine years old as of this writing, has a rare impairment called Central Auditory Processing Disorder and Jan Jr., a year younger, is autistic?

Maureen has had to learn how to work with an educational system that falls far short of its goals. After two years in a school supposedly created to help autistic children, she called a meeting of their teachers and administrator. She asked them if they thought that Lucas could be taught to count to 100, learn the alphabet and multiplication tables and develop some vocabulary. The response: "Oh no, Mrs. VanHoek. Not at this time, but maybe after years of work." They had no idea that Lucas had been home schooled to count to 100 forwards *and* backwards. Furthermore, he knew his multiplication tables, the ABC's, and had mastered vocabulary words through a fourth grade level. Maureen couldn't believe that not one of his teachers was aware of any of that.

One day Lucas had wandered off from the fenced-in school. The administration had provided three aides who were responsible for only five children. When he was later found unconscious by a gardener in a nearby playground, none of the aides was even aware that he had left. Maureen and Jan had had enough. They pulled him out of the school and hired a teacher to come to the house for his education.

They have made the adjustments necessary to continue working the jobs that they love while providing a healthy, loving environment for their sons, giving them as normal a life as is possible. Maureen and Jan both work as much as possible at their home offices. Each of them is required to travel, so they arrange their schedules to insure that they do not both travel at the same time. Jan Jr. has a Special Needs Aide that works with him at home. Lucas attends a special school which is an hour's ride from home requiring four hours on the road for Maureen each day.

Barbie and Ken never had to work two jobs while raising two children with serious impairments. Divorce among parents of autistic children soars above 70%. Of course Maureen and Jan lead a challenging life. They have had some dark times but NEVER felt like they would split apart. They may not have time for date nights or alone time, but they love spending time with their boys.

Challenge wasn't new for them. Two or three months before their wedding, Jan was diagnosed with testicular cancer. Their bond was so close that Maureen had been having anxiety attacks. She kept telling Jan that something was very wrong, though she didn't know what. The day he came home from getting the results of his blood test (required for the wedding license), she gasped when he came in the door. She blurted out, "Oh my God — you have cancer" — before he even told her. He had surgery immediately, and their honeymoon was cancelled for radiation treatments.

Told that they would likely never have children, they were not surprised that, despite trying diligently in the natural way as well as in-vitro, five childless years passed. When Maureen started feeling sick at a business conference in San Diego, everyone told her she was probably pregnant. Arriving at home, she bought a pregnancy test kit, and it came out positive.

Six kits all came out positive! Refusing to believe it, she convinced a hospital to do an ultrasound and, sure enough, there was Lucas.

Things did not go smoothly even then. Maureen had placenta previa, a condition that blocked the uterus, interfering with normal delivery. A new doctor, attending her during an examination late in the pregnancy, was not aware of the placenta previa and ordered an invasive procedure. Shortly after she arrived home, Maureen began to hemorrhage and was rushed to the hospital for an immediate C-section. She spent the next 5 weeks in a hospital bed not moving. Lucas was born 5 weeks early.

Maureen recognizes that, though she may not be skipping in the daisies, we all have our own challenges and make choices as to how we will deal with them. When they got the autism diagnosis for Jan Jr., their second child, it was the death of the dreams for him that she didn't even realize she had. Now it was clear that he wasn't going to be the star of the football team, the prom king, or class president. Rather than dwell on the negative, she immediately reassessed and developed new dreams for him that fit in the new context. Though it took Jan longer to adapt, they did come to the same place of seeing their sons as miracles and huge blessings. Their bond strengthened even further.

Maureen knows in her heart that she and Jan were given these two beautiful boys because they were meant to help them in ways that other people may not have been able to do. At the times when Jan Jr. is in his darkest place, experiencing absolute despair and pain, Maureen taps into an incredible degree of patience that she had no idea was possible. It is this that allows her to be what he needs so that he can emerge from that place. She hadn't known that she had this capacity within her. Now Jan and Maureen are considering adopting other special needs children.

What started out as an incredibly romantic story between star-crossed lovers has turned into a far greater love story encompassing an entire family. I feel blessed to have been able to tell it.

INTRODUCTION TO "THE MIRACLE WORKER OF GHANA"

America is called "The Land of Opportunity." Parents tell their children that they can do anything that they want to do. If they are committed to their dreams, consistent with their efforts, and persevere, they can overcome any obstacles and achieve remarkable things; because they live in a country where all things are possible.

But what chance does a boy have if he is born in Ghana, raised by an abusive uncle after his father dies, runs away at twelve years old with nothing but the clothes on his back and grows up in a small village with no friends or relatives. What chance would that boy have to grow up, get a PhD. degree in Canada, and return to Ghana to realize his dream of helping tens of thousands of people in his native country have a better life? Most people would say that there would be zero chance of that happening.

One boy believed that, with faith in God, even he could see this dream come true. Meet David Mensah.................

THE MIRACLE WORKER
OF GHANA

I met David Mensah when I was in the Peace Corps in 2009. Living in Daboya, a village of 5000 people on the White Volta River in the Northern Region of Ghana, my assignment was to help the weavers create a tourism program. A Peace Corps Volunteer never does just one thing, so I also taught English at the Middle School and Vocational School, helped the farmers learn how to raise cotton, and connected the tailors and hairdressers to regional associations. The fishermen told me that their biggest problem was the annual cost of replacing fishing nets and asked me to help find a solution. It was that request that led me to Dr. Mensah.

What I discovered was a man of seemingly infinite energy who was passionate about restoring vibrant life to the rivers of Ghana. This "River Policeman" had already mobilized a volunteer force of fishermen to eradicate the illegal use of dynamite, DDT, and trawler nets on the Black Volta River. Through his efforts, a lifeless body of water was restored to a place where fish, turtles, birds and other wildlife thrived once again. Now he was eager to duplicate that feat for the White Volta River. When I told him about the challenge being faced by Daboya's fishermen, he enthusiastically jumped on board. He would be happy to work up a plan to decrease the cost of their nets while also providing them with a means for additional income. This neatly fit into a program he could develop, with their help, to eliminate all use of dynamite, DDT, and illegal nets on the White Volta.

I was so impressed with the work this one man had done, and was continuing to do, to improve the ecology of Ghana while making a better life for the fishermen of his country. Then I found out that this was only the tip of the iceberg. Through the Northern Empowerment Association (NEA), tens of thousands of men, women, and especially children are being helped to escape poverty through programs that are designed to be sustainable. Their approach not only reduces poverty but enables people to realize their own value and abilities. Amazingly, the NEA is a non-profit corporation which had been formed by David and some of his friends **when they were high school students**!

I was blown away by the providence in finding this man, who was the key to a problem I was trying to solve, at the exact time that he was looking for a way to make a connection on the White Volta. He was not so surprised. Serendipity had become a way of life for David, and he now saw it as God's will opening to him as he was open to receive it.

This story is all the more amazing when you consider where it started.

The Early Days

David's father died when he was about 11. At that time he was known by his Deg name, Kwabena. He and his older brother Yaw Kara were separated and sent to live with two different uncles in Yaara while the two younger brothers, Yaw Kumah and Kwabena Bichala, were to live with their mother in the distant village of Jugboi. Following a year of severe emotional and physical abuse, Kwabena ran away, making the 40 mile trek to Jugboi where he hoped to live with his mother. It was not to be. Due to tribal social norms and the danger he would place his mother in if his uncle found him there, he had no choice but to make his own way in another village.

Kwabena desperately wanted to attend school and he knew that his cousins went to a school just three miles away in Bamboi. There he went where he was no man's child and, therefore, unable to enter school. He found a small line and hook and would sit on the bank of the Black Volta River fishing, crying and angry that his Dad had to die so early. He only needed one or two fish per day to feed himself. On good days, when he caught more than that, he sold the balance to the market women who were kind to him and paid him one shilling, which was enough to buy sugar and gari, an inexpensive staple food of the area. It eased his sorrow to feel that the fish were sacrificing themselves for him, and it was here that he developed his deep connection to the river and the life that flowed in it.

At this tender age, Kwabena discovered that simply by following his heart and putting himself in a certain position at a certain time the right people would come along to help him. A new-found friend's father allowed him, along with some other school children, to sleep in a room he had available or on the veranda when the room was filled. An old friend of his father's, who lived in Bamboi, claimed guardianship of him so he could register for school. Even though this friend, Kofi Kinto, was a penniless drunk whose wife had to beg for food, he stood up for Kwabena when his uncles came looking for him. He threatened them with police so that they retreated and left Kwabena to his new life. With two pence saved here and there from the money he made selling fish to the market women, he bought the khaki pants required by the school and began his dream of learning.

He entered Class 1 when he was 12 years old, significantly older than the other children in that class. The teacher even had to find him a special table and chair since his legs didn't fit under the tiny Class 1 table. Motivated by his own passion, Kwabena studied hard. He also enrolled the help of senior boys to tutor him in exchange for fish and Kantalaga fruit. Hunting for this sought-after fruit and fishing took up most of his weekends. After a few months, the teacher saw that he was ready to move on to Class 2. His learning was so rapid that he spent only two weeks in Class 2 before being promoted into Class 3.

Though happy in school, Kwabena had nightmares many nights that his uncles would still come for him some day. His fears were visualized as swimming across crocodile-infested rivers while bound in chains and ropes. Frequent rain and ever-present mosquitoes added to the challenges of the night as he often slept by himself outside on an open veranda. Fear came from the packs of dogs that would howl all night long. His most fearful night came when he saw a huge man, larger than any man he had ever seen, approach the area where he lay at about 2:00 in the morning. He had a large cudgel resting on his shoulder, and he was accompanied by a large pack of dogs. He came very close to where Kwabena lay. The boy feared deeply for his life. Fortune, or God, smiled upon him. The man never saw him, nor did the dogs pay him any mind.

Over his final few years in primary school, Kwabena continued wandering from home to home, finding food and shelter where he could. Eventually, another relative took him in and supported him. This man, although generous and a good man in many ways, was steeped in witchcraft; and Kwabena was soon caught up in the power of the dark side of life. His heart became stubborn and hardened, and he fell in with the wrong crowd. Soon, he was the leader of a gang called The Landry Boys. They were brutal and heartless and terrorized their village. Even the police were afraid of them. Though David is now ashamed to speak of those days, it was his gang activity that brought him to God.

Seeing a man speaking to a crowd in the village square, The Landry Boys decided it would be great fun to disperse this crowd by stoning them. They moved into the crowd and waited for Kwabena's signal to start the rout. Instead of giving the signal, he was captured by the old man's stories of Yesu, God's direct son, who had come down from heaven to help humanity. After a sleepless night, he went to the old man to learn more about Yesu and how he might fill the vacuum in his heart. A miracle occurred. Suddenly Kwabena saw all of the evil deeds that he had done displayed on the wall as though projected from a movie camera. Terrified and exhausted, he broke down sobbing and sobbing - the first time he could remember crying since he was a small boy. He knew that his heart had been changed forever. Only compassion and love remained, replacing the hardness and anger that had lived there. This spiritual connection was to drive the rest of his life and bring about the miracles he was to bring to Ghana.

Finding Vision Out of Poverty

At around 16 years of age, the young man found his way to Tamale, the capital city of the Northern Region and, by far, the most populous place to which he had ever been. Here he had no friends or relatives, and life on city streets was dirty, cold, and sometimes brutal. He met many other orphans and saw close up what the scourge of poverty can do to the human spirit. Another young man, who was to become a life-long friend, would go to the back of bakeries with him looking for discarded bread which they would share with others in need. Sayibu had been ostracized from his family when he converted to Christianity from his Muslim faith. Like Kwabena, who was now mostly going by his Christian name, David, he had no family support and was on his own. From conversations between these two orphans came the vision that his life was to be dedicated to helping orphans and the poor. As one who had suffered, he knew what it was like and was, therefore, in the best position to help. David was determined that he would study hard, go on to higher education and one day return to Ghana and to Tamale and help the children. He saw himself building an orphanage with a farm and a place to raise fish. This would allow street urchins, as he had been, to raise themselves up to self-sufficiency with pride. He would be like a father to them and teach them the skills they needed.

Realization of the Dream

In fact, he and Sayibu, with help from many others along the way, would go on to do much more than that. Rather than an orphanage, they created a program to place street orphans with families who had lost children. Each family was given $50-$100 to start a small farm. Though the children he worked with, 10-12 year olds, had learned to be thieves to survive on the streets, they trusted David because of his background. They quickly saw the value of a loving family and honest work. Starting with ten families, this program has now grown to 5600 families and only one child failed, due to dependence on alcohol.

In Ghana, women in their 60's and 70's are often considered witches and are ostracized from their villages, finding their way to Tamale and other cities to beg on the streets becoming, in essence, another type of orphan. Through the Northern Empowerment Association, David initiated a farm project in Janga as an intervention for these women. Here, each woman was given an acre of land planted in peanuts, a crop vital for supplemental protein, and were taught how to work the farm. At each harvest, the crop was divided into three bags: one bag went to the woman to pay for her labor, one was used as seed for the following year, and the third bag was donated to a new woman to get her started. After the program was established, corn was added to the farm. This program began with seven women who were found wandering the streets with glazed eyes, so exposed from starvation that you could count their ribs. Not only did their health improve, but their self-esteem and sense of purpose was restored as they helped themselves and other women as well. From the humble start of 7 women, the program has now mushroomed to include 8,000 women, all of whom are making what is considered good money. Many of them have their grandchildren working for them. This was a huge help to their daughters who were often widowed, having married much older men. These small farms, therefore, have a hand in supporting three generations.

As incredible as those results are, this program has done far more than that. Combining the agriculture (known as "agric" in Ghana) knowledge taught by Dr. Mensah with the intuitive knowledge these women already possessed about weather patterns, nature and seasons, they formed a group called Technical Agric Extension Offices. This group became known in the region as farming experts. Men in the region would come to Dr. Mensah asking for his help in setting up their farms, and he would refer them to this group of women. Initially, the men refused to go to women for help; but when David steadfastly refused to help in any other way, they acquiesced. A striking record of successes resulted in men coming from all over the region, often picking up the women with bicycles to bring them to their proposed farming area. After a time, people stopped calling them witches and treated them as equals. This was a remarkable achievement in this culture.

A similar project, subsequently started in the village of Carpenter, was enhanced by adding the raising of ostriches for their incredibly protein-rich eggs and, also, a Tilapia fish hatchery, which Dr. Mensah was told was impossible due to the harsh climate. Processing of shea nuts, abundant in the Northern Region, added an income of over one million U.S. dollars to the women of the villages involved as shea butter is a sought-after commodity in the western world.

One thing led to another. While starting the agric program in Janga, it became obvious that the people in poor villages also suffered from lack of clean drinking water. Water obtained from polluted ponds often contained disease-causing organisms that significantly threatened the health of the village. While river water was safer, women had to walk two miles with large, heavy water pans balanced on their heads. David organized a program to dig wells. This program was responsible for the creation of 120 fresh-water wells serving many villages in the region. This cut diseases by 75% while, in most cases, reducing the two mile walk to about 50 feet.

As his fishing group grew in numbers, some "converts" grew increasingly aggressive about the mission and developed a hunger for power. He had to remind them that they had once been "bad" fishermen and so needed to have more understanding. He wouldn't let them take weapons with them when they were going to confront fishermen using illegal practices, banning the carrying of even the omnipresent machetes. He only gave them cameras so they could take pictures, allowing the police to later identify the culprits. Dr. Mensah encountered many terrifying situations in the early days of setting up this program, and it called his attention to violence. Having seen the awful role that tribal warfare played in creating and maintaining poverty and a growing number of orphans, Dr. Mensah called the Chiefs of the Northern Region together and created a Peace Program. There is no telling how many lives have been saved as a result of this ongoing cooperation among the tribal Chiefs.

As they say in those late night television commercials, but wait — there's more!! Since 2007, sixty Canadian doctors and nurses and 30 English surgeons have come to Ghana each year as volunteers, seeing 10-11,000 people in a 3-week period relieving intense suffering and saving many lives. Over 300 hernia surgeries alone have already been performed. The doctors pay their own way and bring their own pharmaceuticals.

Getting to the Dream

So how did all of this come about starting with a starving high school student living on the streets of Tamale? That is a story of serendipity, determination and faith in God, and it starts with his feet.

During his years as a street urchin and a thief, running was a skill that he developed out of necessity. When David got to Form 1 in Tamale High School, he joined the track team and excelled in the 800m race. His winning ways in the National Games won his school great acclaim and won him the respect and love of the principal and the whole school. This opened the door for him to work at the school during holidays and earn some money which he put away to go towards the orphanage that had already taken form in his mind. He shared his plans with a young CUSO (Canadian University Service Overseas) volunteer named Alison who had come to speak to the high school students about service. He told her that his dream was to go to an interdenominational Bible College, become a minister, and then return to Ghana to serve the poor. Impressed with the young man's altruism, Alison agreed to check into possibilities at Ontario Bible College (OBC) in Canada. She was true to her word and, in 1979, David's hands shook with excitement as he read a letter from OBC accepting him into their program. Having continued to work at the high school as a lab attendant after his graduation, he had saved enough money to cover his air fare, but just barely. The question of how he would cover his school fees, not to mention eating, seemed insurmountable.

The answer came quickly and easily. An uncle, who also was very excited that David was being given this opportunity, sold a cow to give him funds to cover his school fees and living expenses for that first year. He also pledged to sell a cow every year to support him. He was on his way, well-funded, or so it seemed. Political strife in the form of a coup d'etat led by military leader John Rawlings prevented the transfer of money to him from his uncle. Fortunately he was allowed to leave the country, but he arrived in Canada with only $10 and a small bag of gari in his pocket.

Worse yet, he mistakenly arrived two weeks before the start of the semester so no one from the college was there to meet him. On top of that, he had no place to live and his luggage had been taken off of the plane in England. All of those issues paled, however, when it came to light that the Ghanaian authorities had failed to attach his student authorization paper to his passport. This meant that David was in Canada illegally and a very irate immigration official informed him that he would be sent back to Ghana on the first plane after his luggage arrived in Ontario. Exhausted, deflated, and terrified, David was afraid that his dream might be ending before it even began.

At this point, I am going to refer the reader to the book written by Dr. Mensah himself, *Kwabena: An African Boy's Journey of Faith.* There you will find the incredible details of the people and events that helped him complete his years of higher education. For the purposes of this story, I will simply say that he was not deported and his faith brought to him many people at just the right times starting with a mysterious young man at the airport who helped him find lodging and a local farmer who hired him to work every weekend so he could pay his school fees. That farmer, Gene Paisley, turned out to have a far more important part to play in David's life as his daughter Brenda became David's wife. For now, I will simply touch on some of the critical points of this truly incredible story.

David received his Bachelor of Religious Education from OBC and went on to a Masters program with Acadia University in Nova Scotia and a Phd. in Environmental Ethics and Development at the University of Toronto. At that point, he was married to Brenda, had two daughters, Elizabeth and Deborah, a wonderful relationship with his in-laws, was working as a beloved pastor in a church, and was living a comfortable, if not luxurious, life in a country that had taken him in wholeheartedly. Many people from Ghana leave with good intentions to return after their education but find the order and good life in the Western world too enticing to give up. David was being offered the opportunity of a University teaching position and found this tempting. After all, he had established the Mensah Food and Orphanage Fund in Nova Scotia and could have served the people of Ghana from afar via that organization. He knew, however, that he had to go back and be with the suffering people of Ghana in person to really fulfill the destiny that he knew was his. He would feel tears well up after eating a nice rich meal as visions of the starving widows and orphans came into his mind. Ten of those people could eat on the meat he was consuming in one meal. He might well be their last hope and there was no way he would let them down.

Before marrying Brenda, he had warned her that they would be moving to Ghana some day; and she would be living in challenging conditions. This was brought to the fore again when her father accompanied David on a trip to Ghana to assess the farming situation and, upon return, telling his daughter, "You can't do it. You just can't do it. These people live like it was here way before pioneer times with women carrying water and firewood on their heads. Don't even think about it." When David told Brenda that her father was right, she told him that his love was all that was important to her and that she would support him no matter what challenges lay before them. Looking back now, he sees that she also loves the work they do and is just as determined as he is. Some people say that she is now more Ghanaian than he is!

The Obstacle Course

As you will read about in David's book, the "simple" path that I outlined in a single paragraph above was a heroic journey in itself. Stouffville, a melting pot today, had only one black person in 1979 - David Mensah, an African who was ignorant of western ways. In addition, he fell in love with and eventually wanted to marry a Canadian white woman. How would her family accept him? How would his family in Ghana accept her? Moreover, the funds he was counting on from his uncle never came as the new military government in Ghana refused to let any money be sent out of the country. He was stranded in a foreign country with no means to pay his school fees and living expenses.

Apparently devastating financial, cultural, and administrative issues arose at every step of his journey through each level of his education, yet miraculously one angel after another would show up in the form of new friends, strangers, school administrators, and others to help him along the way.

In 1990, the Mensah family, now including a third daughter, arrived in Accra, Ghana to begin their work. They were armed with an education and a dream but still no funds. With money he had earned teaching and lecturing in Canada, they had bought a small house in Tamale, a pick-up truck, a "fridge", and some basic furniture. Upon arrival in Tamale, they discovered that the Volta River Authority had been renting their house and had damaged it to such an extent that it was unlivable. Ironically, the man who came to help the homeless was now homeless himself. Brenda, David and their three little girls found themselves on the floor of a tiny room in a Catholic Guest House. Without even sleeping mats, they slept on their duffel bags and a pile of the clothes they had brought. Discouragement set in. By the third day, Dr. Mensah had serious doubts about putting his family in this situation. His suggestion that the family leave him and return to Canada was quickly rejected by Brenda who was determined to stay by his side.

Encouraged by his family's toughness and resilience, as well as his own faith in God, David asked where the poorest of the poor lived. They were directed to Janga, one of the poorest and most disease-ridden villages in Ghana. Here he began to set up his farming program but again adversity struck, threatening to end his program before it really got started. This time it took the form of three disgruntled youths who were sure that he had been given thousands of dollars to help the women, orphans, and farmers of Janga but was keeping it all to himself. They quickly spread these lies around the village, poisoning the minds of everyone who would listen. About the time David was again wondering whether he should just quit and take his family out of Janga, other youths in the village met with the disgruntled ones and reasoned with them. If this man has all this money, then why is he even here? Why doesn't he just take the money and run. Why is he wasting his time sharing his knowledge, his ideas, and the little money he has with us? These insightful boys won over the village who could now see the truth. The villagers opened their arms and their minds to receive Dr. Mensah and his ideas. That got the ball rolling and got the attention of the Canadian Ambassador who encouraged David to apply for a Canadian fund designed to help people doing agric and medical work in third world countries. They responded favorably to his proposal, and in 1992 awarded him $100,000.

Saving a River

Remembering his humble beginnings, David traveled to Bamboi to visit the river that had sustained him. As a boy, he would throw his last piece of kenke into the river as a meal for the little red-tailed fish that he loved to watch. Attempting to replicate that memory, he tossed a bit of kenke into his beloved Black Volta River and watched it float for a while and then sink to the bottom as no friendly little fish came to feast on it. This is how he discovered that the fishermen were using illegal methods including fishing with fine mosquito nets that took the fish eggs out of the river along with the fish. There was no life left in this previous source of sustenance from the dam all the way to Lake Volta. Broken-hearted, he tried to talk to the fishermen, but they just couldn't understand that they had created their own poverty.

Determined to restore the river, David went to the EPA, police, and every other group of whom he could think to enlist their help in reversing this trend but was told he was naive and unrealistic. One official told him, "You've been away from this country for too long." Once again, he turned to the poor youth - the very people he had come back to serve. He told them, "God gave this river so that you, your children and your children's children could live on it. Fishing as you do, however, will result in not a single fish or turtle being here for your children." Starting with the few that believed him, his volunteer group grew to 500 within three years. He had gotten the Environmental Protection Council to create a standard hole size for nets. Before the program could be effective, he had to confront the police who had been taking fish as bribes from the illegal fishermen. By embarrassing them at a large meeting, he turned them around. They started to cooperate with his volunteers, arresting anyone identified as fishing illegally.

His efforts were not without peril. He became known as the "River Policeman" and patrolled the river in canoes along with his volunteers day and night, often threatened with guns and machetes. Ator, an influential man among the illegal fishermen was outraged that this man should interfere with their lives and determined to get rid of him any way he could, telling David so to his face. Even Ator, however, was converted when, after 3 years of the program, he saw Nile Perch returning to the Black Volta. With these magnificent fish in his catch, he felt like a rich man indeed. He humbled himself by coming to Dr. Mensah and telling him that he used to hate him but now understood that he was a good friend to the poor fishermen and had brought them prosperity. He begged forgiveness and pledged to support the new program with all of his strength and fight anyone who would speak out against it. When David looks back now at the dangers and the hardships he endured to initiate this program and celebrates with Ator now as he puts his children through school with money he has earned from fishing, he feels peace and joy in his heart.

Healing the Sick

Seeing illness all around them, David and Brenda knew that they were also being called to serve in this arena. Neither of them was medically trained, and there were no resources within Ghana that they could bring to the table. Enter Jennifer Wilson. She and Brenda had become fast friends during school days in Canada, and now she had become a doctor. They had spoken many times about Jennifer traveling to Ghana to see for herself the kinds of diseases that they dealt with there. She finally came with a few friends, and it opened her eyes to a world that shocked her and spoke to her compassionate heart. She received incredible response to a notice that she sent out to Christian doctors and nurses in Canada asking them to come on a mission. In addition, while on a flight, Jennifer happened to sit next to Andrew Kingsnorth, one of the top surgeons in England. Seeing the African shirt she was wearing, he asked if she knew a way that he could go to Ghana to see if there was a need there for hernia surgeries, his specialty. Amazed at this "coincidence," she connected him to David. When he went over on an exploratory visit, he found hernias everywhere he went! This was particularly an issue for farmers as it rendered them unable to work their land.

Thus was born the medical program described at the beginning of this story. David worked with the Minister of Health and the Director of Medical Services for the Northern Region to establish a training program for Ghanaian nurses which was hugely successful. Currently, they are planning to build a hospital with hopes that it become a model for future rural area hospitals - a place where people can be treated by a "real" doctor and get the highest quality of care.

The Final Chapter

The final chapter of this amazing story is still being written. Dr. Mensah's dream continues to expand the boundaries of ways that he, and those that work with him, can help people escape the ravages of poverty. When I originally asked David what his passion was, he told me that he loved to combine passion, perseverance, consistency, and commitment to accomplish things that others say can't be done - particularly as it comes to helping the poor abandoned by those with better resources. He longs to teach the youth of his country that resilience and tenacity are even more important than skills and education when it comes to shaping a productive life. He also wants them to know in their hearts that God will always be there to help anyone who is trying his/her best to help humanity.

Postscript

Well into his sixth decade of life, Dr. Mensah often misses meals or eats cold food as he works tirelessly on his projects. He says that the more that he sweats, the better he sleeps, knowing that he is doing the unimaginable and doing it well. The Northern Empowerment Association (www.grid-nea.org) was started by high school students who were themselves mired in poverty yet fired up with a dream to help the poor people suffering in Ghana. This association now employs 117 full-time people in addition to about 60 members of women's groups part time. This is in addition to the 550-600 volunteers involved in the fishing program. The NEA also coordinates the healing ministry of the doctors, nurses, and surgeons that come every year from Canada and England. Thousands of poor people have been helped medically. Thousands of women have been saved from the stigma of being perceived as witches and are now respected, successful members of society. In addition, thousands of children have been removed from squalor and put through school, and thousands of farmers have improved their health and, thereby, their productivity. On top of all of that, the Black Volta River ecology has been restored to a healthy state so little boys can once again drop a hook and line into the river and catch tilapia while enjoying feeding those little red-tailed fish.

The fascinating details of the transformation of Kwabena to Dr. David Mensah, which I have only touched on in this story, can be found in *Kwabena: An African Boy's Journey of Faith*, available on Amazon.

INTRODUCTION TO "LITTLE GOURMET SON"

I LOVE to eat! Probably one of the reasons I married a gourmet cook, although there was also all that red hair, the big eyes, and.............but then, that's another story. Not only do I love to eat, but I also lived in Phoenix, Arizona for 30 years. Say what you want about TexMex and CalMex, the BEST Mexican food in the U.S. is in Arizona. OK – I'll give credit to New Mexico, which I have to rate up there with Arizona. Truth is, they do some dishes even better than Arizona, especially having to do with chilis.

Which brings me to Chile Rojo. Let me be clear that I am a Mexican food snob. When I would go to Rhode Island or Minnesota or even San Francisco or New Orleans and someone would say, "I know a great Mexican place," I would always find a graceful, or sometimes not-so-graceful, way of steering them to another option because I KNEW that it was not going to measure up to my standard.

So, here I was in Puerto Viejo, Costa Rica with a group of friends going into a restaurant called Chile Rojo. Right away I was curious because this is an odd name for a Costa Rican restaurant. My curiosity grew when I looked at the menu and saw Thai Green Curry Chicken, Fresh Yellow Fin Tuna with Thai Ginger black bean sauce, and a Middle East Vegetarian plate. This was DEFINITELY not a typical Costa Rican restaurant! Then I saw that they were having a special that day: Chicken Quesadilla. Knowing that it couldn't be anywhere close to my beloved Arizona variety, I decided to order it anyway because it had been a long time since I had a chicken quesadilla and even a pale imitation of the real thing would be a welcome change from rice and beans.

OMG!!! This was NOT as good as Arizona – it was MUCH better! This was not even food made on this planet – not even in Mexico! I was speechless (a very rare occurrence) and beyond joy. I wanted to marry the chef – who was a MAN!! I absolutely could not believe how good this dish was so I *had* to meet the creator and owner of this restaurant. Not surprisingly, I met a man who also loved to eat and had the name to prove it. From this love of eating, he found his bliss in life: cooking and watching people enjoy his food.

Meet Andrew Bacon...................

"LITTLE GOURMET SON"

as told by Andrew Bacon

"Little Gourmet Son." That's what my father called me from the time I was only four years old. He could hardly know that he was predicting my future, my passion, my life.

My father was an executive for Mobil oil, so our family travelled the world. Born in Nairobi, Kenya, I moved to Hong Kong when only 9 months old. Upon first meeting our new Chinese cook, she snatched me right up and declared, "We'll look after that one!" That was really the beginning of the development of my international palate. For more than two years, I ate only genuine Cantonese food and fell in love with it.

This presented a problem for my parents when we moved back to Kenya when I was three, as I refused to eat anything that was **not** Chinese food. Seeing an opportunity here, my older brother Michael took me with him to catch flying termites. Convincing me that this was a Chinese delicacy, I proceeded to pop them right into my mouth. Much to his surprise, I loved the taste and texture so much that I convinced Michael to eat them as well! Both of us were hooked!

I did, of course, learn to eat African food. In addition I became particularly fond of Indian food which was plentiful, as there was a large Indian population in Nairobi. My mother was an excellent cook. She would make Indonesian chicken satays which Michael and I devoured. We would sit on the beach and compete to see who could eat the most satays. Though he was five years older, I managed to hold my own in those contests.

From the time I was four, Dad had taken me on trips with him. We ate in fine restaurants, and he never asked for a children's menu for me. By five years old, I was eating oysters on the half shell and other delightful specialty foods that other children wouldn't touch. This is when he started calling me his little gourmet son.

As I approached nine years of age, Dad was transferred to Paris, which opened up a whole new world of gastric delights to me! We would go to a new restaurant every week and try new things at each one. I was entranced with French cheeses, seafoods, frog legs, and so many other new flavors and textures. I marveled at how people could create such wonderful dishes in such a variety of ways.

About two years later, we were transferred to Sierra Leone and culinary disaster struck in my life. Feeling that the schools in Sierra Leone were inadequate, my parents sent me to English boarding school. The English may well have a superior educational system, but food is not high up on anyone's list of reasons to go to England. Then again, English food is not half bad when compared to English boarding school food! While for most students, this may have simply been part of school life, for me, it was pure hell. I lived for holidays when I would go home to my mother's wonderful Indian, French, Indonesian, and Thai treats. Sierra Leone is also where I was introduced to Lebanese food which is very common there. This is a taste I retain to this day, and I'm guessing I'm the only restaurant in Costa Rica featuring Lebanese dishes.

By the time I was fifteen, and somehow still surviving English boarding school food (and I use that term loosely), another transfer brought the family to Sudan. When I returned home for those longed-for visits (both to see my family and to eat wonderful food), I was introduced to French/Arabic fusion, as our cook was a French-trained Arabic man. A new taste for me to savor! This, plus our one-month holiday each year in France, was enough to keep my great love for food alive and well.

Discovering The Business

When I was 18, my Dad retired. Following a short time in Kenya, the family moved to Vancouver, Canada while I went on to college in England. As a young student, I envisioned myself winning Pulitzer Prizes as a great writer. Didn't take long to discover that dyslexia does not a great writing career make. Not even my teachers wanted to read my work!

Still, if my passion had been to be a writer, I'm sure I would have found a way. As it was, my passion was food. I had always loved eating fine foods. By this time of my life, I was thrilled to discover that I had a real talent for re-creating many of the yummy dishes I had been enjoying all of those years. The really good news was that I didn't need to know how to spell to excel at cooking!

A short-lived study of hotel administration led me to working in a hotel in the tourist resort town of Kelowna, a bit northeast of Vancouver. That begot a job in a French restaurant where I found deep inspiration from the French owner who was totally passionate about serving people good food. In the 80's, flambé was popular so I received extensive training in that approach.

I moved on to an apprenticeship in a Vancouver ethnic restaurant named Kilimanjaro under the tutelage of an amazing Indian man named Amin Sendaji. Amin had been raised in Uganda, and this got me back to my African roots. All of the food was supplied by Indian vendors except for the vegetables, as everyone knew that the Chinese had the best vegetables. Since only Indians worked in the kitchen, Amin had me start as a floor manager out front. Seeing my exuberance for cooking, which I made no effort to hide, and my deep knowledge of ethnic dishes, Amin finally relented and added me to the kitchen staff. The uniqueness of this was underlined one afternoon when our Indian supplier of Nan bread pulled Amin aside and incredulously asked, "What's the white guy doing in the kitchen?" In an attempt to save face, Amin replied, "It's okay. He's African."

By the time I was 25, I had extensive knowledge about Indian, Indo-African fusion, and other ethnic dishes and decided to try out my wings and open a restaurant in the countryside outside of Kelowna. Working with an experienced chef as well as a good friend who was attending a culinary school, I added deeper knowledge of classic European food to my skills. A wide array of Continental dishes was joined with the exotic flambe dishes I had learned in the French restaurant. Being the owner, I needed to learn all aspects of the restaurant business. Being in the kitchen, however, was what really made my heart sing, so I eventually took over as executive chef of my own restaurant. Amazingly, the Canadian government recognized me as a formal chef (even though I had never been to a culinary academy!) and sent people to me for training.

I had realized my dream of not only creating exquisite dishes, but also of watching them bring great pleasure to others, as they had to me. Now I wanted to get more into the heartbeat of the city so I closed my countryside restaurant and opened a new one in the midst of Kelowna. People flocked to my theme weekends where I matched music (another love of mine) to specially-prepared dishes reflecting African, Reggae, Blues, and Jazz themes, among others. This return to my roots of African, Indian, Thai and other ethnic foods was wildly popular but the combination of increasingly-rising costs and a steep downturn in the economy led me to close that restaurant.

What was I to do now? Well, I had explored the foods of many cultures. Why not be a part of some of those cultures to develop a deeper resonance? Having a real love for chili peppers, especially as used in Mexican dishes, this seemed like the perfect time to enhance my relationship with a cuisine I had not yet mastered. Off I went, backpacking in Mexico for six months, to immerse myself in the Mexican culture. This included a six-week cooking course in Oaxaca.

Finding Heaven

Mexican – African – Indonesian – French – Chinese – Thai – European – Indo-African Fusion – Lebanese – French-Arabic Fusion. Such an exquisite palette of tastes, fragrances, textures, and visual delights. My greatest desire was simply to gift people with these dishes, interacting with them personally, and seeing them surprised and delighted with the results. How could I best do this?

Enter into my life the Maple Leaf, a 107 foot ecotourism schooner that carried 18 guests and 4 crew between Vancouver and Alaska. My role was simple: do whatever it takes to provide the guests food that they raved about, and don't serve the same dish twice. Combine that with a blank check to buy the finest ingredients, and I had found Chef Heaven!! Here was a place that I could bring all my skills to bear and develop new dishes of my own as I had sole responsibility for both menu selection and all of the cooking. I also got to be up front and personal with all of the people I was feeding on a daily basis. Even after the guests went home, I would get fan mail from them!

As if that weren't enough, there was another aspect of the Maple Leaf that inspired me in terms of how I wanted my ideal business to work. Imagine a working environment where EVERYONE loved what they were doing. This was the Maple Leaf. Of course the guests were ecstatic. They were whale watching, visiting villages they had only read about, seeing bears and other animals close up (well – not TOO close to the bears!), and having photo ops they hadn't even dreamed of. On top of that, they were on a fantasy schooner and enjoying the best food they had ever eaten. So their joy was a given. Beyond that, everyone I worked with had the same passion and love for their job that I had for mine. The captain couldn't imagine a finer life than sailing. The first mate (who was the captain's wife) also loved being at sea and working next to her husband. The deck hand felt like an actor in a movie driving the Zodiac and knew that life couldn't get any better than this. I had never been around passion like this in a restaurant working environment. Having experienced this slice of Heaven, I was now determined to recreate it in my own restaurant when the time was right.

In the off-season, the Maple Leaf went to the Sea of Cortez in Mexico. Same ship, same crew, same job, but a WORLD of difference! In the waters off Alaska people power-eat! Just trying to stay warm invites massive consumption and a desire for "hot" foods. In the warm waters off Mexico, breakfast is usually just toast and tropical fruits, lunch might be ceviche, guacamole and chips, and dinner is a salad and firing up the BBQ or maybe eating the lobsters the guests just dove for today. It's actually more challenging to come up with varied menus when most people only require light meals. This helped me develop another aspect of the culinary arts.

Remember my desire to live in the culture of foods I so dearly loved? Well, during the seven years I worked on the schooner, I had time off and spent stints traveling and studying food in North Africa, Central America, and Thailand. Finding myself with 6 months free one year, I took a season's wages and went off to Bangkok with a copy of Lonely Planet under my arm to get thoroughly familiar with the Thai food so dear to my heart and stomach. On the plane, I made the ill-advised decision that I needed to be completely open to eating everything they served over there. After all, I was accustomed to exotic foods; and I knew that if others enjoyed these cultural dishes, I certainly could. Bristling with confidence (read, arrogance), I strode into a restaurant and told the owner that I wanted the food served the same way that the locals eat it. Overcoming his objections that it would be too spicy for foreigners, I declared, "No, no…just bring it on. If you can eat it, I can eat it!"

Yeah, right! Within a week, I was spending half the night on the toilet clutching my stomach and hoping I might die before morning. Trust me when I tell you that you do not really know hot food until you have eaten genuine Thai food. For the first time in my entire life I actually considered the possibility that I should just stick to pasta with tomato sauce like the other tourists. Of course, part of that may have had to do with the aging process. As a 20-something, I had a cast-iron stomach that could handle anything. It's possible that all of the fiery goodies I welcomed back then had eaten some holes in that cast iron!

Most people never experience one Dream Job in their lifetime. In my early 40's, I found my second. A millionaire investment banker who loved gourmet foods hired me to be the private chef on his yacht. Again, I had a blank check, and this time I was only cooking for 4 guests, the captain, and myself. With his money, I bought cookbooks from some of the world's best chefs, the finest ingredients, and top-of-the-line implements. I turned out elaborate feasts with fine wines that I could never even have thought about affording personally. My goal was to cook something every day that I had never cooked before. I had discovered another neighborhood in Heaven!

The Next Chapter

Even though I loved what I did, don't think it wasn't hard work. I cooked 5 meals/day, 7 days/week, for 5 months. With luck, on any given day, I might catch an hour's nap during the afternoon. After nine years shipboard, I took my wages and headed for other places I wanted to visit. With my significant bankroll, I lived like a king in Africa and Central America. This was, however, more than just R&R. At 44 years old, I was tired of living out of a backpack with no home or relationship. It was time to put down roots and, at the same time, create my dream restaurant. Where to do it was the question. The U.S. and other developed countries had systems that were too complex and required an investment that would call for partners. I was determined to do this my way without strings being pulled by financial backers. I wanted to be by the ocean in a tropical area where it was affordable.

My first choice was Thailand. What, however, would I offer there that was different for the local population and attractive to tourists? So, I started traveling through Central and South America. I loved Mexican food but to own a business there, you have to have a 51% partner who is Mexican. Not happening! Continuing my journey, I found that the further south you go, the worse the food gets!!

In 2002, I arrived in Puerto Viejo, Costa Rica. Not only was it a tropical area on the Caribbean, but I found that I could grow everything that they grow in Thailand. Interestingly, nobody in Costa Rica used those ingredients in their foods. In fact, every restaurant in the area that wasn't serving hamburgers and pizza to the tourists had a menu that was pretty much limited to rice & beans and the local casado plate with rice, beans, fried plantain, salad and fish, chicken, or beef. With an ample tourist population of Americans and Europeans, I knew I could be successful here.

All I really wanted was a cozy, small restaurant that my daughter Gina and I could create with a handful of tables and a relaxed life style. That was fortunate because the funds I had available just matched my dream! At least I thought of it as my dream. Others may have called it a 5 x 7-meter hole in the wall restaurant with 7 tables and a kitchen smaller than a decent walk-in closet. No unlimited checkbook here. I started with a roof that leaked, a dining room that flooded with every rain, and a household stove and fridge that I had hauled down from Canada in an '89 Toyota pickup. To open each day, I had to drag two corrugated iron garage doors off their hinges, across the sand, and deposit them on the lawn. Working in the kitchen brought to mind Dante's Inferno, which matched the theme of the 6 wildly bright colors that it had been painted when it was a Columbian restaurant. The only, but very important, redeeming factor was that I could rent this Taj Mahal for only $300/month.

Fortunately for me, Gina was with me. She had just graduated from culinary school and moved to Costa Rica to be with me. Not only was she a huge help in the kitchen but she also had an artistic flair that I was sadly lacking. We repainted the walls white, and she sponged in subtle yellow highlights and trimmed the dining room out in blue. Still looking like a dump from the outside, at least we were no longer garish on the inside.

Now, what to name our palace of culinary delights? I had had a restaurant in Panama which I had named El Ultimo Refugio (The Ultimate Refuge). I rather liked that name but realized that it was too hard for people to remember. I wanted something that would paint an instant image in people's minds. Having always loved chilis, I decided on Chile Rojo (Red Chili) and came up with a sexy, attractive logo. Apparently this worked because, even today, people who have eaten in my restaurant will call out to me, "Hey, Chile Rojo!"

The Obstacle Course

You've probably heard the conventional wisdom that it takes 3 years or longer for a restaurant to be successful. Forget that! We were packed from Day 1 with lines of people waiting to get in. Why, you ask, would a dumpy looking place with broken-down chairs be so successful? Well, it didn't take long for word to get out that there was a place in town that was serving different food from all the rest. A place where you could get five star hotel dishes at a fraction of the cost.

So, yes, we were wildly successful but not wildly profitable, as all the money we made was re-invested in the business. Back then, we only had to pay $1/hr for experienced help and .80/hr for others, but we still strained to make payroll while trying to improve the restaurant. The first couple of years took enormous determination by me and Gina. Fortunately, stubbornness runs in our family! In Puerto Viejo, break-ins and robberies are commonplace, and we had our share. We had to deal with frequent power outages and water shortages since the city only provided us with a single pipe. That certainly wasn't enough, even for our small restaurant. Every night, I would fill a big storage tank, but I would invariably run out of water the next day. This meant trips to the sea every day to fill a large garbage can with water so we could flush the toilets. In addition, I averaged 10 trips every day to my house to fill 2 buckets with cooking water.

I know what you're thinking – why didn't I just make one trip and bring more water? Remember that '89 Toyota pick-up that I drove down from Canada? I had bought that truck for $1800. The Costa Rican import tax was $2000! Eventually, the police figured out that I wasn't just passing through, so they impounded the vehicle since I wouldn't pay the tax. So, all of these water runs were on a bicycle!!

Another major hurdle was that we were operating without a liquor license which would have cost $12,000 – certainly not in my budget! When four big Americans come in for lunch on a hot day, the first thing they ask for is a round of beers. No beer – no customers. Not wanting to lose the business, it was not outside my code of ethics to serve beer in coffee mugs. That, unfortunately, had limited success since jealous, rival restaurant owners with empty tables would keep an eagle eye out and suddenly police would show up checking what was in those coffee mugs!

I found out that I could rent a liquor license from an existing owner for $250/mo, and I managed to find such a benefactor. Getting approval, however, proved more challenging than I had imagined and took six months. The inspector kept coming up with reasons to block my license. First he said I didn't have enough tables. Then it was not enough indoor tables. Then not enough bathrooms. Then the toilet was too close to the kitchen. None of these made any sense as restaurants in the area with similar situations did have liquor licenses. I went to the owner of the license, and he assured me it would be no problem. We just needed to take a 2-day jaunt down to see The Man where the regional authorities were located. We journeyed there on a weekend, went to the man's home, had dinner with him, spent time with his family, and then, as suggested by my coach, I slipped him a little envelope with a bit of cash in it. The Man graciously told us to come to the office Monday morning. Lo and behold, when we did, everything was signed and ready to go. Problem resolved and my naivete gone forever. Now I knew the envelope approach to getting things done with the Costa Rican authorities!

Then there was the day that I got a bit careless while dragging those corrugated iron gates across the property. They cut the power line, which was buried just inches under the sand, thereby fusing two 110v wires together so I suddenly had 220v into my kitchen. I found out quickly that light bulbs don't handle 220v well! Sounded like gunfire with all those bulbs exploding before I could throw the main switch. Being too obstinate to close the restaurant, I ran a long extension cord from the chicken place next door. Since that line wouldn't run both the blender and the stereo, we had to shut the music off every time I made a blended drink! I converted the fridge to an old-fashioned ice box with a big block of ice. I counted myself lucky that my stove ran on gas. We got the electricity back up the next day, so I would have lost only one day's business if I had shut down; but Gina and I preferred doing whatever we had to do to stay open that day. What a day!!

It would have been nice if that had been our only challenging day, but by now you've seen the pattern. We had "interesting" days all the time. It was only my dream, my vision, and my hard-headed stubbornness that kept us going.

<u>Moving On</u>

By our second season in 2004, we had managed to squeeze in 9 tables and then expanded by adding 4 large tables on the back lawn. We had built a thatched roof over those tables so the tourists were fine in the frequent rains, but our staff got soaked as they ran back and forth serving meals.

That year the cavalry arrived in the beautiful form of the woman who would become my wife. I had met Ikuko in Vancouver in 2000 and our attraction grew. In 2004, she came to visit me for a holiday and never went back to Canada. She immediately jumped in and was a huge help to me and Gina. Just in time, too, because wages and other expenses were climbing. The owner had his own dream – knocking down the buildings on this site and building a shopping center. He had included me in those plans, promising that I could open my dream restaurant as part of that center. My immediate challenge was that he was not willing to put ANY money into fixing up the existing site, so I had to pay for all repairs and improvements including electrical, plumbing, and tile.

In 2005, he told me it was time to build the shopping center. He was going to raze the old restaurant and in 6 months the shopping center would be up and ready for me to launch my new restaurant. Hooray!! I was thrilled until I did the Costa Rican math. Six months = 18 actual months on any construction project. I knew I couldn't afford to lose everything I had built up by being out of business for that long, so I made the decision to move to another location temporarily.

I found a beautiful location with eleven tables across from the beach. Unfortunately, the building did not match the beauty of the location. As we repainted, retiled, and rewired the electrical system, I sometimes wondered if the ceiling would come down on our heads! It leaked so bad that things spilled on the floor of the restaurant above us dripped down on us. We had the same water problems as the old restaurant. Fortunately, we were right across from the sea; and we also used a barrel to catch rain water. Even with all of these issues, we still did an incredible business. With Gina doing breakfast and lunch, me doing dinner, and Ikuko helping everywhere, we would serve 50 tables before noon and another 50 in the evening. Good thing, because the rent on this place was $1000/month!

We expanded by putting a table on the beach. Of course, that was illegal since it was a public beach; but the customers loved it. It gave us an edge since no other restaurant had beach-side tables. We added a second table, and then a third, and soon we had six tables on the beach. We had the unbeatable combination of the unique Chile Rojo cuisine and beach dining. At least, we had that for four months until the government cracked down, and we had to pull off the beach tables. Still, even without the beach tables, we did a remarkable business during the interim period until the shopping center was built. Now I finally had an opportunity to design a restaurant where the ambiance could match the food.

Chili Rojo in 2014 and The Future

The struggles of the past are not visible in today's Chile Rojo where you can enjoy an alcoholic beverage with your lunch or dinner overlooking the main street of Puerto Viejo in a beautifully-styled establishment. Some things don't change, though. I wanted to open before Christmas 2007. Government offices, however, were closed so I couldn't get inspected. Somehow, it was just fine to open in December and have the inspection in January after I "fixed a couple of envelopes."

Chile Rojo does not draw the local population. On any given day, you'll hear German, French, English, Italian, Dutch, and Spanish. We have 18 tables, reliable electricity, no need for bicycle trips to get buckets of water, no leaks in the roof, beautiful décor, and no iron gates to drag. I must admit that I miss the days when I only served the dishes that I loved to cook. Over the years, I expanded the menu to please the tastes of a wider range of people. Oh, we still serve the exotic and varied menu for which Chile Rojo is known, but some more mundane dishes worked their way onto the menu as well.

Having a restaurant is an extension of yourself through the food you serve and your translation of styles and ingredients. In the last several years, I have studied healthy, organic foods and have begun growing my own herbs. The vision for extending my dream is to actually go back to having a smaller restaurant where we will serve organic, healthy foods and grow a lot of the ingredients myself. We will become more exclusive, offering only the signature dishes that I myself love, create and cook. Being smaller, I'll cut down on the administrative end and be able to spend more time interacting with every customer that walks in my door. Though the form has changed several times and will change again, the vision stays the same: it's all about the food and the people – that's what I'm passionate about.

PostScript

In 2015, Andrew in fact, moved Chili Rojo again and it morphed into a more intimate venue just as he had envisioned. He traded in the cushy chairs and Western-world feel for a more genuine, rustic Caribbean motif.

Cutting back to just 12 tables, you could say he has come full circle, only without the leaking ceiling, flooding dining room, and daily water runs. He only moved 1 1/2 blocks, but it's a whole different world. Instead of being upstairs in a mall environment, he is on a street corner right across from the beach. He has cut back his menu, eliminating the Americanized items like Tex-Mex and other dishes that he never enjoyed making and added fresh, organic foods to his exotic, imaginative dishes. Diners watch him walk across the street and pick up Red Snapper and other fish directly from the fisherman as they pull their boats up on the beach. Often, people will order whatever fresh catch they see in his hands.

Interestingly, his business has increased 100%, even with fewer tables, as he is getting faster turnover and more consistent business right from opening at 11:30 am through to closing at 10 pm. In addition to his tourist trade, Costa Ricans have begun to come experience this friendly restaurant with the unique menu. Another advantage to the cozier setting is that it is much easier for him to staff appropriately. At the larger location, he often had more staff than he needed or looked foolish and unprofessional when he had too few people to handle a sudden rush.

Ikuko is still working by his side, while Gina has married, moved to Colorado and now has a five-year-old son.

Oh - and those iron gates? They're back, sort of. He no longer has to drag them across the sand but he has given up his remote control from the upstairs restaurant and now has to close the gates manually. If you find yourself in Puerto Viejo, you might want to make a special effort to get there before he locks those gates for the night.

INTRODUCTION TO "FINDEN HIMMEL"

All too often, people change their geography hoping their problems will disappear with the new scenery but we all know the saying, "Wherever you go, there you are." Your location is rarely integral to your problems or your bliss.

But rarely is not the same as never. Just as there are certain activities that seem to be part of our Divine Design, there are times when a location appears to be part of our DNA and provides the right setting for our bliss to blossom. For some people, that might mean the ocean, the mountains, the desert, or the forests. Many people have risked everything to come to the United States, the land of opportunity where the streets are paved with gold, so they could make their dreams come true. There are times, however, when the dream cannot be born in the United States. There are times when those born here are drawn to another place so that their passion can go from ignition to full blaze.

Meet Anne Fuchs........................

FINDEN HIMMEL
(FINDING HEAVEN)

as told by Anne Fuchs

<u>The Lie</u>

I didn't know.

I really didn't know how miserable I was.

I had a decent-paying job with good benefits and worked with some really great people. I had a loving family. And I was singing! My heart's dream was to be a singer, and I was doing it so all was right with the world. Or so it seemed.

The fact is, I had built up a happy façade for those around me. Maybe I even believed it at times. Truth? I enjoyed the people with whom I worked for the most part, but the job was unfulfilling and depressing for me. I was going through relationship after romantic relationship with the same bitter ends and hurts, tearing apart my sense of identity and my belief in love all together. My family IS loving, but I felt oppressed by their strict religious observance. My Dad is a deacon in the Catholic Church, and my mom is deeply faithful; but as much as I admire their connection with the spiritual world, the specificity of the regimen is deeply empty and unsatisfying for me. I can't connect. Even my beloved musical life, while varied, was frustrating as hell. It felt as if I were running around like a guinea pig in a wheel feeling unappreciated and unworthy.

I was a woman who was inwardly losing my mind. I was going to weekly therapy sessions to work on my "snapping" issue and to work through an explosive fight I had had with my sister. I was literally trying to fill each and every second of my life with something to do so that I could feel some sense of purpose. I had developed a pretty severe rash on my face for a while, and I was breaking out in eczema all over. My car was broken into, I was getting traffic and parking tickets, and the ensembles with whom I was singing seemed to be socially "shunning" or phasing me out, somehow. It was literally as if the universe were giving me every possible sign to make an enormous change.

The Vision

I was fortunate that a good friend and co-worker gave me two books to read - *Creative Visualization* and *The Art of Possibility*. Thank you, Phyllis! I don't know if you had sensed my misery or if you are simply an ancient, wise woman, but those two books saved my life. I started to journal, to envision, to focus in complete detail on the life of my dreams, which was certainly not the life I had been living. In my perfect world, it became clear that I would be living in Germany, speaking German fluently, singing on a German stage, riding a bicycle everywhere, drinking beer in biergartens, and meeting lots of new people.

The crazy, crazy thing is that when I put this intention into the universe, I see now that it literally did manifest itself in my life. Piece by piece, my life began to reflect my thoughts. I began to do the things that would make it possible for me to follow my dream and my heart. As I made the decision to move to Germany, I vowed to adopt a "no stone left unturned" mentality towards my life. To me, this was more than a bucket list. It meant living without regret, DOING the things that I imagined, and, hopefully, leaving this planet knowing that I had exhausted and experienced every possibility that I had dreamed of instead of settling for less.

When I think about my life in Germany now as compared to what I knew in America, I see total fulfillment, even in its imperfection. It was a pure decision that I made on my own, outside of the eyes of my family, my friends, and even the love of my life. I decided to be extremely "selfish" and to do what I really, truly dreamed of, and just let myself completely fail at it if need be. I couldn't go on dreaming of what could have been or could be. I just had to KNOW.

<u>So How Did I Get Here?</u>

> *"Until one is committed, there is hesitancy, the chance to draw back, always ineffectiveness. Concerning all acts of initiative and creation, there is one elementary truth the ignorance of which kills countless ideas and splendid plans: that the moment one definitely commits oneself, then providence moves too. All sorts of things occur to help one that would never otherwise have occurred. A whole stream of events issues from the decision, raising in one's favor all manner of unforeseen incidents, meetings and material assistance which no man could have dreamed would have come his way. Whatever you can do or dream you can, begin it. Boldness has genius, power and magic in it. Begin it now."*
> Johann Wolfgang Von Goethe

Goethe was a pretty smart Dude, AND he was German! You might say that the serendipitous events that started me along my path to a fulfilled life started with the Army. If my sister's husband hadn't been stationed in Ansbach in 2001 when they got married, I might never have discovered how much I loved Germany. Other critical elements included opera's requirement for German, my voice teacher's husband, Pittsburgh, and crazy Mitch Painter. There were jobs that fell into place in Germany, people to help with my visa, my guardian angels Gertrude and Heinrich, and so much more that I never could have planned or even imagined. But I get ahead of myself. Let's start with the summer of 2006, my sophomore year in college.

As a music major, I had to study languages. Though many students find learning languages as much fun as chewing on tin foil, I was thrilled to find that languages came easily to me, especially German. So off I went to Germany for a summer immersion program. I was blown away to find out that the head of the program chose little ol' me to live with his family. Their adorable three little girls instantly became my best friends and, as they spoke NO English, my best German teachers. "Coincidentally", they were also taking piano lessons. Through their piano teacher, I was introduced to opera conductors. Next thing I knew, I was sitting back by the harp watching one of these men conduct a program at a festival in Austria. The same night, I was watching accordion players in a chamber ensemble doing a crazy production of "Don Pasquale"!

It was amazing! All the reasons that I had felt that I just didn't fit in when I lived in the U.S. vanished, and I felt at home here. More than that —- I felt vibrantly alive and passionate about my life. The possibility of having a singing career in this magical land set my heart on fire.

<u>Why Germany?</u>

I don't know.

Maybe my heritage had something to do with it. My grandparents came from Germany. It's true that I wasn't really aware of that growing up. My family never celebrated German traditions or even knew how to speak German, but that doesn't mean there might not have been something going on in my DNA that was calling me in that direction.

During my first trip over, for my sister's wedding, I fell in love with how clean and organized everything was, the cute little SMART cars, and the **totally-**cute boys who just seemed so much older, more mature, and cooler than American guys. Speaking of the "cool factor", I could drink beer at 16! As far as beer is concerned, I have only one word — JEVER. This beer is supremely awesome, cheaper than water, and a total Nordwest Deutschland thing. It doesn't even give me hives, raising my happiness factor another notch. Doesn't get any cooler than that!

On subsequent trips over, as I got older and just maybe a bit more mature (although I have friends who would question that), I found there were things at a deeper level that were drawing me to Germany.

I was never comfortable with the American pristine approach to opera. I felt like I was visiting a museum where people were almost afraid to even dust the artifacts for fear they would be damaged. I felt such insecurity in the opera world there. In Germany, the music was alive with new possibilities. The performers made it their own, and conductors were willing to take risks. I saw a pretty cool production of Carmina Burana, and it was truly awesome. The Germans turned it into something of a Bavarian wonderland, with Dirndl-wearing, deer-horn hanging, bier stein-holding frauleins decorating the stage and provocatively bouncing their curls (and booties) to the beat of the erotic springtime music. The entire percussion section was bedecked in Lederhosen, and there were Bavarian images projected all over the place. The chorus even passed around some bells and beers in the middle of the whole thing. It was really creative and fun.

I knew that THIS was where I had to be to sing opera in a way that released my soul.

OK – I admit that some of the other reasons I preferred Germany may have been heavily influenced by the fact that I was spending time in the urban northeastern part of the U.S. where the culture was all about cars, malls, politics, pollution and the American Dream. Well, I didn't want the American Dream, at least not the one that says you can have it all if you'll just work 60-hour weeks and keep up with the Joneses. I don't even know anyone named Jones!

The life I dreamed of was one where people sat around the dinner table for 4 hours enjoying conversation and being comfortable with the silences in between. Where people actually enjoyed being with each other without having to check cell phones and iPads every 5 minutes to see if they were missing anything. Where people were more concerned with doing one thing at a time and doing it right rather than being in an ADD frenzy to see how many things could be multi-tasked. I wanted to safely walk or bike home, even late at night. I wanted to get from Point A to Point B using my body as a means of transportation and smell clean, fresh air on the way while passing well-kept homes in which people took pride. I wanted to live, to enjoy living, to make it my business to be someone who was proud of living her life.

Touching The Dream and The First Big Dilemma

Along came the summer of 2009 and an opportunity to attend a 3-month, international training program for opera singers at the Lyric Opera Studio of Weimar. We had students from America, Germany, Holland, England, Africa and France. They had set up an entire program of rehearsals and performances. They brought in agents to evaluate us, and our shows were televised locally. Oh my God – I was singing opera in Germany!! This was incredible! I wanted to stay here, move here, live here. How could I make this dream transform into permanent reality? Having just received my Masters from Westminster Choir College, I had no job waiting for me at home, no husband and children waiting for me, no reason at all to return to the U.S. I could do this! I could stay here!

Then my left brain joined the conversation. My upbringing, one of six children, came to the fore.

Anne – you are a responsible person – one who takes her obligations seriously. You need to stand on your own two feet. Are you really going to be this selfish? Chasing some silly dream when you have things to take care of at home? You're not a child anymore. You are an independent adult. Act like one!!

Actually, that's the tape that was playing subconsciously. Consciously, as I sat in my room in Weimar, there were only two words in my mind; but they were lit up like a Las Vegas marquee: **SALLIE MAE!** Those student loans weren't going to disappear just because I was singing arias in Weimar. I convinced myself that I had to go back, find a real job, pay off those loans and really get my act together.

The Lost Years

I often wonder what might have been if I had told my left brain to shut up. It was ironic really, because nothing dramatically changed by my going back to the U.S. in 2009. Sure I saved up a little money by living with relatives and finding some temp work; but with the Obama Income-Based

Repayment Plan being applied to student loans and my making less money than a decent street mime, I wasn't required to make payments anyway.

I did discover that my dream wasn't going to die. It was always with me. While singing in a cabaret in Times Square, New York City, I could feel my feet standing on an opera-house stage in Berlin. While doing temp work at a law office in Trenton, my heart was visualizing auditions in Weimar. While on a date, I was thinking of how quickly I could get to Germany rather than whether I had a future with Bob. I AWAYS felt like I had one foot on the plane to Germany and was living a half-hearted life.

The nice thing about that law office was that most of the people there really supported my dream. The boss was a music lover and a few folks from the office would come see me perform. I kept my music alive doing opera, contemporary, chorale, cabaret, theatre, church music, chorus work. Hell – I would have sung on the street corner if nothing else came up! I did auditions in NY, Philly, and NJ and took whatever gigs I could get.

Still, I entered a black period that drove a stake into my heart and almost killed the dream that lived there. A relationship I started with an American singer I met while in Weimar went toxic. He was bitter about opera and kept telling me that I wasn't nearly good enough. That was supported by the trickle of gigs I was getting while doing seemingly endless auditions. Some of those auditions were totally embarrassing and my self-esteem was in the toilet. I finally had an audition where they were really excited about my voice, and then I heard the words of doom, "Can't wait to see you at the dance audition!"

Some would say that I'm an average dancer, but only those that love me and haven't seen me dance. I suck! Thirty singers showed up at that dance audition in a room too small to hold fifteen. None were trained dancers. We were faking our way though it trying to impress a Broadway choreographer with our bright smiles and tight asses since none of us could dance. We were clunking around like the NY Giants offensive line trying to do ballet. Still, as bad as the other 29 were, I was worse and didn't get the part. At that point, I was preparing myself for a career as a clerk in a law office.

Then came 2012 and three crazy things coincided to breathe life into my dream and propel me back to Germany.

Lois Trevor had been my voice teacher for four years when I was in undergraduate school at the University of Kentucky, and she was a huge influence in my life. She is the one who taught me how to express and convey the *spirit* of the music I was singing: to sing from my heart and not just from my diaphragm. Her husband, Hans Froehmmer, had been an agent but quit after they were married. Lois passed away in 2008, and he decided to resume his agent activities focusing on Germany. He contacted me in May and was sooooo excited about helping me start my career there!

A month later, I was accepted into an eclectic singing program in Pittsburgh that included all of my interests: opera, musical theater, cabaret, and contemporary music. Totally immersed in the world of music again, the flames were fanned BIG time, making me feel that deep hunger. I again KNEW that this was all that I wanted to be doing.

As if on cue, Mitch Painter called me out of the blue. Mitch was a really close high school friend who was currently singing as a full-time tenor in the Oldenburgisches Staatstheater in Oldenburg, ... you guessed it – Germany! Mitch is one of those friends who knows me so well that he can speak the unvarnished truth. He knew how much I longed to be in Germany and he called me out.

Anne – You know you want to be here so stop all the bullshit excuses and just dive in!

When I told him that I had to have some way to make money, his reply was graphic and emphatic.

*I'll get you a f***ing job! Now get your ass over here!*

And he did! He got me a job at a language school teaching English and also let me move into his place until I could get established. How could I say no?

Taking The Plunge

In case I hadn't gotten the message already, the universe seemed to conspire against my continuing existence in the USA in the form of hurricane Sandy along with a near attack by a Kujo-like Rottweiler. OK – I get it!

So I gave up my cushy.........well, OK – maybe not cushy but at least stable.................law office job with great benefits, let go of my angst about Sallie Mae (well, maybe not ALL of my angst), said a tearful goodbye to Brandon (more on the love of my life later), told my left brain to take a hike, and spread my wings to fly into my fantasy life.

You might have thought it was more nightmare than dream if you saw the spiffy living conditions I moved into. Good thing I came to Germany with only two suitcases because Mitch's apartment was so small, I had to go outside to change my mind! Mitch had cut a mattress in half (barely the size of my body) so that it could fit on the floor behind his door, which was still a step up from having to sleep with Mitch!

I thought I'd be off to a roaring start because my agent was on fire. He had sent letters ahead and set up several auditions. Having read fairy tales, I should have known that the protagonist needs to taste defeat before victory. Then I wouldn't have been surprised that none of those auditions translated into gigs.

There were so many auditions where I heard the same thing: "You are good – just not quite good enough". After a while, it sounded like a recording stuck in a broken loop. I managed to land a one-on-one class with a major, famous soprano followed by a week-long class with her along with 5 other students. I thought that was great until reality hit. God – she was hard on me. I felt like a marine in boot camp. She even told me that I flat didn't know how to sing AT ALL!! So you can imagine how astonished I was to find out that she had set up an audition for me at the end of the week with her agent! I was as nervous as a virgin bride on her honeymoon, and my voice just wasn't ready for the music they selected. To top it off, the agent was completely turned off by my stage presence and the way I moved. She actually said to me, " Don't move. I can't stand looking at you! JUST STAND THERE AND SING." God, I was so embarrassed and discouraged.

It didn't help any that Oldenburg was having its darkest, dreariest winter in 58 years. It made Seattle look downright sunny and bright. The rain just kept coming, and it was often reflected in my dreary mood. My lowest point may have been getting tips on how to sing from a Siberian string player.

All this time, I was still holding my breath because I didn't yet have my work visa. Here in the lovely land of the Deutsch, there exists one magical hour in the day, between 11am and 12pm, four days per week, in which an Auslaender desperate for a work visa, such as myself, has both the obligation and privilege of phoning the Auslaenderbehoerde and speaking personally to a disgruntled employee whose job it is to make appointments to pick up that very special piece of paper when it is sitting on his desk.

In my case, I was waiting with baited breath (whatever that is) for the official permission for Anne Fuchs to work in Germany as both a singer and a teacher! Alas, in vain, I called and called, every three minutes for an entire magical hour every day, my heart sinking millimeter by millimeter (we are in the metric system now, after all) when SUDDENLY, at 11:58 a.m. on a magic day, lo and behold, a beautifully-disgruntled voice greeted me in German and made my appointment dreams into a reality! O joy!! O rapture!!! Perhaps this is a sign that I can make this happen after all.

Prior to that victory, the only way I kept going was because of the support I was getting. My Mom prayed for me a lot, and we skyped all the time.

Anne – You just do what you feel right about and follow your heart.
I skyped a lot with my agent back in Kentucky also.
Anne – You're fine. Keep pushing. Don't give up. I'll take care of you. Just keep going. ***Don't let them take away your confidence.***

My friend Phyllis and others from the law office kept encouraging me also. Then there were the friends I had met in Germany. June, a fellow singer, always had my back. Susan, from the language school, was my #1 cheerleader. Greta, a German actress, helped me with my German and was a big help with the bureaucracy. Then, of course, there was Painter. Mitch is one of the most unique, extroverted, funny, and fun people that I have ever met. We were fast friends when we were 16, having found a common ground in both loving opera and wanting to be opera singers. After all this time, being so close to the dream, there was NO WAY he was going to let me quit.

The author of this fairy tale began writing the procession towards the happy ending. It started with one of those stiff, awkward Northern German dinner parties where everything was oh so appropriate and perfect. Can't say it registered high on my fun meter, but it was good to meet some people. Towards the end of the night, I was asking the hostess if she knew where I might find an inexpensive apartment as Mitch's floor was getting old fast. An older couple at the table overheard us. Gertrude and Heinrich were Guardian Angels disguised as Germans! They told me that they loved my story, my courage, and what I was doing and invited me to move into their spacious home rent-free for as long as I liked. They even told me they would love it if I would sing all over their house! Goodbye tiny mattress – Hello beautiful digs!

Host mommy and daddy were so good to me in every way. Together we fought our way through the German bureaucratic jungle. We tackled every language barrier until we reached today's level of what I can finally call fluency. I tasted every traditional German dish under three suns….. including the famous, traditional northern German "grünkohl". Mama and Papa Steen even threw a big party for all my theater friends!

Maybe a week after my move, I got a call from the theatre where Mitch worked (he still loved me!), and they offered me the role of Papagena in the Magic Flute. I'd love to say it was because they were blown away by my brilliance, but the driving factor in this decision was that the woman who had the part was taken ill 2 days before opening night! When asked if I could learn the entire part in two days, I gave a resounding and excited YES and went into panic mode immediately upon hanging up the phone. TWO DAYS TO LEARN AN ENTIRE OPERA!!!! Was I crazy? Well…. Yes, I was. It almost killed me, but I did it, and I must have done it well. They brought me back several more times and, then, offered me a contract for a German Operetta in the Nov, 2013 – July, 2014 season. YES – The dream is alive and a reality! I'm in Heaven!

How Could Life Get Better?

Not that I'd want to bitch about Heaven, but there was one small thing missing from my TOTAL dream. Every fairy tale has to have Prince Charming. This one was no different. I met Brandon during that magical time in Pittsburgh. Maybe it was the music. Maybe it was his boyish charm and killer smile. Hell – I don't know – maybe it was something in the Pittsburgh water. Whatever it was, I was smitten BIG TIME and so was he. Who knew there really was love at first sight?

He was not only my true love. He was also the SECOND BIG DILEMMA.

We loved each other and wanted to be together. My dream, however, was a crescendo in my brain and in my heart and I couldn't possibly ignore it anymore. What's a girl to do? Brandon was kind, sweet, and handsome. He was also very talented and extremely fun to be around. Most important, he just understood me. He was also wise and loved me enough to let me go.

We both know you'll live a life of regret if you don't grab this opportunity now, Anne. Go for it. If what we have is real, it won't die. Follow your dream, and I'll support you 100%.

But the story wasn't over when I kissed my handsome Prince and fled across the water with tears in my eyes. The writer of happy endings was all over this one. Two months later, Brandon came to visit and just couldn't leave. I did my best Mitch Painter imitation and got Brandon a job at the language school and let him move in with me (by this time I had my own apartment). Needless to say, I didn't make him sleep on the floor behind my door!

I'm not saying it was all roses and chocolate. We had six rocky months that may have been one of the most trying times of my life. Money, new culture, learning the language, losing and finding jobs, work visas, total uncertainty, rough edges, and, oh, did I mention MONEY! There were ultimatums on both sides, but we found that our love was true. We have grown stronger and closer through it all, and now I can say Heaven is complete.

I think I know a bit about what that is now. My "bliss" doesn't mean that I am ecstatically happy every single day of the week. No, not at all. I still have challenges and hard times, but *I chose them.* I can honestly say that, from the second I arrived, I have never doubted my decision. Even when things were hard, I had never felt so free and so good. I have never had less money in my life, and I've never been happier. Every day that I am in Germany, I am inwardly completely fulfilled and satisfied because I *put myself there.* I did the riskiest thing I have ever done, and I willingly rise to the challenges of each day. I sing on the German stage as I always dreamed I would. I speak German fluently as I always wanted. I teach English, which wasn't in my dreams, but which fills my life with joy and fulfillment, as well. The cherry on top is that I have the love of my life by my side while I do it, even when the chips are down and things are hard.

No challenge seems insurmountable because I filled my life with love and decided to direct love outwards into all my activities.

Goethe was right. Once I was totally clear about what I wanted, it was *so easy* to make it happen. Somehow my loved ones wanted to help me to get there, even though it would mean a separation. It was so beautiful. Reminds me of another Goethe quote: "Trust yourself and then you will know how to live."

I hope you can understand what I mean when I say that for the first time in my life, I feel like I could actually die and be ok with it. I know it is a strange thing to say, but I feel it somehow. There are, of course, more dreams forming, more ideas and more goals, but the biggest dream of my life is realized. I am finally, finally content and truly at home.

<u>Postscript</u>

Anne was right when she said that there were more dreams forming. Just as she couldn't predict the amazing journey that took her to Germany, she couldn't possibly have imagined the next phase in her life.

Her contract with the theatre ended July 20, 2014, and around the same time her white knight fell off his horse. She thoroughly enjoyed the wild ride of following her bliss even though she ultimately discovered that she did not want the everyday life that came with it. She found herself going to auditions without the burning desire that used to fill her heart and was surprised to realize that she didn't care if she got the job or not. She had painted a picture of what her dream would look like but when she entered into that picture, it just wasn't her.

When her parents came to visit her in November and saw that she was no longer on fire about being in Germany, they invited her home and she knew that this was the right move for her. Brandon graciously agreed to finish out their lease and take care of the closure details.

Following a crazy odyssey that saw her eating the head of a pig in Slovenia on New Year's Day and acting as a translator for a German construction crew in Canada for six weeks, Anne returned to Indiana on Feb 15, 2015. Somehow, that chaotic and confusing transition was what she needed to process the grief of losing her fairy tale come true of singing opera in Germany with her dream man by her side. Unbelievably, she was back in Mishawaka, Indiana in her parents' house and her only connection to her beloved singing was what seemed like a failed resume. To stay sane, she prayed a lot and kept herself really busy.

But she also kept her heart open and when you do that, strange things happen. Like a visit to Great Clips. Not even for herself. She went to keep her dad company when he went to get a haircut. There she met Joe, a friend of her father who also was a master in sacred music and organ performance and the Director of Music at St. Bavo Catholic Church. They just happened to be looking for a cantor for their music program. Taking that job put Anne in touch with the mayor and other city council members who let her know that they were looking for someone who would be willing to chair a Heritage Festival committee. This would be a festive gathering of cultural music, dance, food, and history, celebrating the immigrant and cultural roots of Mishawaka. The mixed cultural background included German along with Belgian, Italian, and other ethnic groups who had settled in the area. She loved the whole idea and came on board as the festival chairperson.

Anne's passion rose again and filled her heart. Who would have thought that her path to bliss would take her from the opera stage of Berlin right back to small town America? Yet here she was with a deep desire to help people find their roots much as she had via her time in Germany. It was all connected in some mysterious way and now she felt a strong attraction to a town filled with people whose grandparents spoke only German, Flemish, or Italian.

Another funny thing happened. Anne discovered a love for America that she hadn't had before she left. Though she had deeply connected with the German people, she realized that, no matter how good her German got, she could never really be one of them. She also had seen how her American friends sacrificed their families, culture, traditions, and a big part of themselves when they married into a German family. She couldn't imagine not celebrating Thanksgiving with her family every year. She saw how much she treasured the vast diversity that is part of American culture. The homogeneity of the German way of life can be very comforting but it stifles any attempts to live outside the box and let creativity fly. Whereas Americans think it's interesting and cool when someone takes a 90 degree turn from what their life path had been, Europeans don't understand it at all.

Following this new passion involved the same crazy, wonderful, serendipitous type of adventure that had brought her to Germany. Who knew she'd be having dinner at the Belgian Club with the mayor and learning to play Rolle Bolle, an ancient bowling game? A woman she had met in a Young Professionals Group came on board as a volunteer and she connected Anne to a man who designed their web site and is doing all of their promotional materials at no charge. All of her non-work time is now devoted to auditioning music acts, meeting with providers of food and beverages, attending committee groups, visiting organizations with the mayor, and infecting volunteers with her own love for this project.

Oh yes - Anne is still singing but now it is in church, at weddings and parties and odd gigs like singing with a 30 piece accordion band doing a fund raiser for disabled vets in South Bend, Indiana. Opera is an amazing, passionate hobby, but now she knows that it is not her career. Singing from her heart, without the pressure of having to get every note exactly right, is what allows her love to flow out and touch all who listen to her.

Lessons learned in Germany:

* What makes a place "home" is the people and there are good, kind people everywhere.
* It's OK to have nothing to say and feel comfortable in your own skin. You don't have to try and be something you are not.
* Being present where you are allows you to build community.

Oh - and one last lesson: Dreams are wonderful and should be pursued but they may not last forever. The journey to bliss may have many stations along the way. Anne is looking forward to what Life will bring her once the Festival is over.

INTRODUCTION TO "CREATING THE GARDEN"

Have you ever met anyone who felt like they were just not part of this world? Some people naturally have a vision of something finer. They're not sure if it is an ancient vision of Life as it was millennia ago or a vision of a future that is yet to be — or both. They know that this vision is their true home. They feel deeply that they are destined to put form to the vision so that others might know it as reality.

Having that vision can be hard to bear. Some know that they can't live in this world, yet they can't find the way to create the new world. That can end tragically. Some are convinced by those around them that there is no such place, and they give up the vision. Theirs is an unfulfilled life. Occasionally, one of those people has the strength, the patience, the wisdom, and the loving heart to create that new world here on earth.

Meet Susannah Light....

CREATING THE GARDEN

as told by Susannah Light

Five acres of tropical jungle and pastureland. That's what most people would see. "How beautiful and serene" they might think, yet they would not see what I saw. I saw a garden. Not simply a garden for growing good wholesome food or dazzling flowers with butterflies and hummingbirds, although those elements would be present. No, I saw a garden where people's souls would be nourished. A garden where people would grow past the dualities now known on earth, past the war of religions, sexes, and traditions that had kept humankind separate from their Divine Truth. You might say the Garden of Eden, though not a reversion to something long gone. Rather, it would be a rising up into something alive and meaningful today.

Tears streamed down my face as I stood on this precious land — land that was in my name, but I knew that it didn't belong to me. None can really "own" our beautiful Mother Earth. The stunning fertility and vibrancy of greenery, rivers, wildlife and spiritual vortex that spread out before me are a gift beyond compare. More than anything I wanted to share this land with many others in a community of kindness, respect, love, and an understanding of true Oneness.

The tears were because this seemed like an impossible dream. I had no resources, a husband who did not support my vision, and no clear path before me as to how to bring this garden forth. That was in 2007. My story and my dream began much earlier.

How it Started

I was raised in a Mennonite family as the second youngest of twelve siblings on a farm in upstate New York. Everyone, including the little ones, always had responsibilities. All eight of my older sisters gravitated towards men's work. One got her license as a tractor-trailer driver and others became cow hands, able mechanics and heavy equipment operators. I, however, was always drawn to my mother's side in the kitchen. Just as well because I was in seriously poor health which prevented me from doing strenuous manual labor anyway. When I was thirteen, I took on primary responsibility for the household when my mother traveled to Belize for several months. This is where my passion for serving others was kindled and burst into flame. Rather than just cooking and cleaning, I saw that I was creating a warm, safe, sacred space for my family's hearts, bodies, and palates. I yearned to provide a beautiful home, pleasing to the senses, that welcomed people into a warm, comfortable setting.

Though there was always a certain tension in the household due to Father's strict religious practices and emphasis on sin, Mother was my role model for creating a safe, calm, caring environment. She was a very tender, upright soul who made sure that we were all cared for and happy. She was the one who guided me in the way to care for a garden, make love the special ingredient in anything that I cooked, and embrace the home and even our clothes with tender devotion so as to create a loving surround. A household with twelve siblings can be a place of jealousy and animosity; but Mother taught us that each person deserves our respect, and that we should delight in one another. She herself was the perfect example of selflessness and a desire to make others happy. We would all meet each night in the living room after chores were done, faces and feet were washed and fresh clothes were donned. Many a cold night she would share a blanket and cuddle with me or one of my sisters in front of the wood stove as we shared tea and, when we were lucky, a huge bowl of popcorn.

I vividly remember an evening when I ran to select a chair that I wanted for myself at our dinner table. Mother simply said, "Ah - Da groB ich und das klein du" (she primarily spoke German). It translates as, "Ah - The Big Me and the small you". That gentle lesson of honoring the value of others versus thinking first of myself entered deeply into my psyche and became one of my guiding principles.

My father taught me the value of work, an appreciation for excellence, and the importance of stamina — how to finish a project without concern for aching bones and tired bodies. He would always say to us, "See to it that what needs to happen happens." My brothers and sisters were tireless on the farm, working all night, if need be, to finish planting thirty acres of corn or getting 1200 bales of hay in before an impending rain hit. If the baler broke down, Nathan and Chris seemed to work magic to get it going in time to get the job done. After working hard all day, my older sisters would sometimes get up in the middle of the night to give me a foot rub or back massage when they knew that I was in pain from my illness. They taught me compassion and selflessness through their loving actions. My spontaneous response was one of deep reverence and the desire to express my love for my brothers and sisters in whatever ways that I could. My sisters also taught me competitiveness. We were always trying to outdo each other to see who could do any particular task the absolute best way it could possibly be done.

Expanding The Vision

I am so thankful for my earthly family for many of the principles that I learned and the love that I knew. Yet our religious beliefs put us in a narrow little box. I had blinders on throughout my youth and early adult years, believing deeply that all who were not a part of the "one true church" were going to hell. Taking blinders off when you don't know that you're wearing them can be an impossible task. In my case, it took extreme measures.

I had severe mono when I was twelve followed by intense arthritic pain in my bones, limiting my movement. I developed fibromyalgia when I was only fourteen and was in fairly constant pain through my 30's. Though it may not have been obvious to people passing by, there were days I couldn't even get out of bed. At other times, I'd wake up screaming with pain in the night. In my 30's, I developed chronic fatigue and endometriosis requiring several surgeries.

Looking back, I believe that my other-dimensional guides were trying their best to get my attention. They were showing me the disconnect between the path of peace and Oneness that I subconsciously knew was true and the doctrine of condemnation and separation that I had accepted. None of it was enough to rip my blinders off. Then, in 2004 when I was 38, I was diagnosed with breast cancer. When my mother had been taken from me by that same disease just one year earlier, I wished that I could die with her. Now it looked like my wish might come true.

Two factors came together in the Atlanta clinic to which I went that knocked my blinders off and brought my awakening to the Truth. One was the fact that I was so totally depleted mentally, emotionally, physically, and spiritually that I didn't even have the energy to judge. All I could do was lay helplessly in bed, aware of the second factor — the loving care that I was getting from people who hadn't even known me. I had no family or friends in the area to support me, yet I don't know if I ever felt more loved.

Since the clinic had no overnight facilities and I had no family in the area, my primary doctor took me home with him every night. The warmth I felt from him and his wife and daughter was astounding. In the clinic, and subsequently in the hospital in upstate NY where I had major breast surgery, I couldn't even think. All I could do was feel, and what I felt was the incredible kindness and love supporting me from every direction - the nurses, doctors, chiropractor, surgeons, massage therapists. It didn't matter what church they belonged to, if they believed in a Christian God, or if the women wore tight, immodest clothing and makeup. When I regained enough strength to think clearly, the thought that filled my mind was, "Surely these amazing emissaries of love can't all be going to hell."

The blinders were off. This final illness had opened my heart like never before. I could see a whole world of love. Condemnation and judgment were gone. The deep desire to serve and care for my family was now freed up to include everyone. This passion was to become the cornerstone of my dream. Ignited in my heart, a clear vision had not yet started taking form in my mind. Just now being exposed to this brave new world of non-judgmental love, I had much to learn.

Finding Costa Rica

Let's back up a few years. For reasons that could be a story unto itself, my father wanted to move the whole family out of the U.S. His desire to explore tropical locations coincided with my doctor's advice that my health would improve in a warmer climate. In 2000, I was sent to live with a Mennonite family in Costa Rica so that I could see if there was suitable property for us to farm. What an adventure for this little Mennonite girl! Learning the language from a dog-eared dictionary that never left my side, I spent two months there by myself learning the bus system and traveling around the country. I fell in love with the land and culture of Costa Rica. I asked my brother Nathan to come for two weeks and help me look for a farm to which our whole family could move. The fruit of our labor was the purchase, in the following year, of the perfect property for us. It was an amazing 100 acres of rolling hills, streams, pastures, tropical forest, and the confluence of two powerful rivers. It had previously been a macadamia orchard that had failed and was now overgrown with many dead trees. Nathan, his wife, two-months-old son and a young nephew joined me as the first members of the family to relocate permanently. Over the next two years, others followed so that in 2003, twenty-seven family members had settled in our new promised land.

I had found a land that already seemed to be in my heart. It was on this land that I discovered the depth of my love for working with Mother Earth — weeding, preparing the soil, planting seeds, and harvesting fresh food with which I could make delicious meals. All around me were happy people, happy dogs, happy chickens. I was in Heaven.

Our family experienced a few good years in Costa Rica; but they were challenging times and finances were tight. Following Mother's death in 2003 and my leaving for cancer treatments in the US the following year, the family divided. What once was a unit of peaceful agreement scattered into factions — brother against brother and sister against sister. All but one went back to the U.S. — some to Virginia, some to Texas, some to

Pennsylvania and some back to NY. Though the land was divided up amongst us, with me receiving five acres, Barbara was the only sibling to stay in Costa Rica. Along with her husband, she worked the dairy farm, making butter, milk, cheese, ice cream and yoghurt to sell.

Shortly after my recovery, I returned to Costa Rica. I opened an ice cream shop, selling Barbara's ice cream, in Puerto Viejo, a tourist town on the beaches of the Caribbean side. I was back in my beloved country and so loved serving people ice cream every day and seeing how much they enjoyed our delicious product. After a year, I went back up to the States and married Gary, a dear friend of our family who cared for me deeply. We went back to Costa Rica and worked together in the ice cream shop for another year. Gary was not convinced that this was the life for him, however, and when our shop was broken into, that was the last straw. We sold the business and, in 2007, moved back once again to the U.S. The last time I had gone back with a broken body. This time, with a broken heart. Leaving the land I loved, I honestly felt that I would never be happy again.

<u>Two in Agreement</u>

Gary and I moved to Sunrise Ranch, a spiritual community of about 85 people in Loveland, Colorado at the foothills of the Rocky Mountains. They had a wonderful 3 1/2 acre organic garden there, and I poured my love into the soil, the food, the mountains, and the wonderful people that I met there. I was surrounded with loving people and great blessings from the earth but, idyllic as it was, I felt a great sadness with the realization that my Costa Rica dream was all but dead.

Wanting to honor and share the Spirit of God as I felt it in Mother Earth, I created Divine Nature Tours, starting with a weekend Retreat in the Rockies. That was expanded the following year into a nine-day Costa Rica Retreat, allowing me to share the country that I loved with people who had never experienced her. These turned into times of reverent appreciation of nature as we spent blissful hours on beaches, trails, and national parks. We enjoyed walking on Costa Rica's mystical land, rafting on her magical waterways, and even flying over the treetops of her enchanting cloud forest on zip lines. These were more than vacations. People's hearts cracked open as they heard the voice of their own soul and learned things about themselves that cannot be accessed in any other way. Each time I brought a group to what I really considered my home, my heart would fill with love and passion, and I would hear my Spirit tell me that this **would be** the birthplace of the garden village that I had envisioned. Following that thought, the tears that I talked about at the beginning of this story would always wash down my cheeks as I could see no clear path to fulfilling my dream.

That all changed in 2012. It started with tears of heartbreak and frustration. I approached someone at Sunrise whose wisdom I respected and asked, "What does someone do when they know something is real but see no way to get there." Her words are still clear in my mind: "Keep on talking about your vision. Someday you'll tell it to someone who will help bring it to life." That someone was my shamanic teacher, David.

He had asked if he could camp on my 5 acres in Costa Rica around the time of the end of the Mayan calendar. He felt deeply within him that Costa Rica was a place of significance and where he needed to be at that time. He was totally taken with the beauty of the area. After being there for three months, he wrote to me, "Your family didn't buy a farm. They bought a National Park!" He also felt that the great spiritual significance that he had sensed in Costa Rica was centered in my property. Finally, someone shared my passion for this land and the possibility of something vast happening there!

Gary and I had divorced (in a beautiful private ceremony on top of Pike's Peak — a place very special to us) earlier that year, acknowledging that we were following different paths. This freed me up to move back to the land of my heart. David and I moved down there even though my land had no house on it. Fortunately, another American owned a home just a bit down the road from my property. He was going to be in the States for a number of months and agreed to let us live in his house in exchange for David rebuilding his roof.

It is said that, with two in agreement, all things are possible. My dream was reborn and, with David's input, magnified beyond my initial vision. Naming the property Garden Village, we formed a non-profit educational program called the School of Sacred Earth Technologies. We would invite young people to come as interns. David would teach carpentry and sustainable building techniques while I would teach permaculture and food preparation. Both of us would provide spiritual training through our example and our counseling. We were excited about the vision but there were two major obstacles in the way:

1. Being land-locked, my property had no road access and, therefore, no way to bring water or electricity to us.
2. We had almost no funds between us.

What we did have was passion and commitment. We watched as miracles unfolded before us.

A neighbor had a six acre property abutting mine and extending to the road. By the time we heard that he was selling it, he already had a buyer lined up; and we had no way to come up with the funds necessary to purchase the land anyway. Nevertheless, David and I knew that this land was to be a part of Garden Village. We had continued to create and give life to our shared vision and discuss it with many people who we knew would be supportive. A financially successful friend loved our concept and agreed to invest in our project, giving us a $45,000 advance. Though he later postponed further investment, he agreed that we could keep the advance as a donation. At that same time, the proposed buyer of the land adjacent to mine pulled out of the deal and our $45,000 was enough for us to make the purchase. Now we had eleven acres with road access, though we still didn't have the funds to begin developing the property.

Being an environmental inventor who had already designed and built the Strawjet — a home-building innovation (www.strawjet.com) and is currently working on the railplane (www.railplane.us), David had a connection with the Ashland School of Environmental Technology. Donations that came in through them enabled us to process the necessary permits and erect our first structure on the property. Appropriately, we called it the "Seed House". Of course, by that time, I had already planted four garden beds and began growing our own beans, broccoli, squash, red beets, and collard greens along with a corn field and banana trees.

<u>Giving Life to the Vision</u>

My original vision hadn't been something that I could clearly articulate in a way that people could visualize and tangibly feel. I often felt the presence of a serene, wise, Divine woman simply sitting on a rock or fixing food from the natural gifts of the earth. This image of Holiness connected me to the Divine Feminine, represented to me by Mother Mary. It drew me into an internal experience of the original state of Being represented by the Garden of Eden — that tantalizing tale of sacredness, serenity, and wisdom. I knew that this was an integral part of who I was, and yet for years it seemed unattainable and, in that sense, unreal.

Adding the Divine Masculine essence, represented by David's creation of new technology designed to protect the Earth Mother, brought the vision into balance and allowed us to begin to add meat to the bones. We were now physically creating a place where friends, accessing the very roots of their Divinity, could work, play, build, and grow food together. Having healed or released the wounded baggage of millennia of strife, we would be able to create a haven of peace and possibility.

We put out an invitation to young people to come on an international work exchange program to learn sustainable gardening, crafts and building approaches that enhanced the Earth instead of harming her. With very little marketing, they began to come and, with their help, Garden Village expanded.

As of the Fall of 2015, Garden Village has added to the original Seed House a large structure named the Leaf House, reflecting the leaf design of its roof. In addition, we built The Cabin, a car port for our trusty old Toyota 4Runner, a carpentry shop, and the Guest Room. The Guest Room is under the same roof as the Seed House. Whereas our original interns in 2013 had only hammocks and backpacking tents, we now have created three sleeping rooms with beds in the Leaf House. Also under the Leaf House roof is a hot shower, a kitchen with a four burner electric stove and oven, a three burner gas stove, a sink with running water, a refrigerator and plenty of beautiful, hand-made counter and cabinet space.

The Cabin is a stand-alone building designed to be quarters for one person or a couple. It features a unique Earth Bed, designed by David, to allow the occupants to remain grounded to the earth while still sleeping on a comfortable mattress. This building was our first shot at what a cabin might be like for someone moving onto the property. We gained valuable experience in how to do similar construction in the future. We are also wide open to anyone who moves here to design and build, or have built, accommodations to their liking. Several locations on our eleven acres are suitable for homes. There is also an area we feel would be ideal for a larger community building.

In addition to our early crops, we now harvest yuca, malanga, okra, lemons, tangerines, bananas, beans, cucumbers, peppers and numerous types of greens. In only our third year since planting those first gardens, we have already had more than two dozen interns come and spend time with us — some for just a few days or a week and some for several months. Some have come back and brought friends. Some have spread the word, resulting in their friends coming on their own.

Our interns are usually in their late teens and early twenties, though we have also had some older than that. They tend to be people awakening to a realization of something much larger than they have seen in the world around them. This has led them to travel and explore both the world and their own inner landscapes. They are free and powerful Spirits with explosive creative energy and an underlying desire, or even urgency, to make changes in the world. They come full of hope and vision of something new and better, free of the existing patterns of stagnation. When they arrive at Garden Village, they are met by two people who are totally committed to bringing a new day of higher consciousness through the expression of love, responsibility for the whole, and an openness to universal intelligence. Here they find a world where it is possible to escape the old paradigm of greed, duality, and separation and enter an evolutionary flow that is congruent with the highest vision coming from their open hearts. They find a place where all are resolved to tune into the wisdom of Nature and work cooperatively, rather than competitively, with each other and Mother Earth. We replace electronic stimulus and distraction with personal connection and interaction. We work with the natural rhythms of the garden and learn how to live on the land in a way sustainable for the total ecology while being healthy and joyful for people.

Fulfillment

My experience at Garden Village is already exceeding my early dreams and has given birth to greater, more expanded dreams. It has given me the opportunity to fully manifest the Mother energy that has been so strong in me ever since my days of my youth. I have been able to teach a new vision of living in a moment-by-moment relationship with nature in a peaceful, harmonious way with those around us. People find it credible because they see me providing a personal example. At the same time, how wonderful it has been for me to hear and receive the hearts of young people and to give space for *their* guidance to blossom.

I have had many spiritual mentors in my life who have taught me how to look beyond the physical world while still living in it — how to be *in* the world but not *of* it. I began learning about meditation, prayers, and expanding my consciousness into the higher planes of Being in Lillydale, NY, the largest center of spiritualism (healers, seers, mediums, and prophets) in the world. It was through this training that I became aware of my guides in the astral planes. This is particularly true of Mother Mary who has been an integral part of the development of my vision of Garden Village. My awareness of higher consciousness was expanded during the five years that I lived at Sunrise Ranch, an intentional community that has been in existence since 1945. There I studied the teachings of Lloyd Meeker (known as Uranda) and Martin Cecil. Their stated purpose was the regeneration of the human race under the direction of the Spirit of God. They taught a larger understanding of God than that with which I had been raised. Theirs was a loving God that was present in all rather than confined to a few. One of the most important aspects of the New Day of Consciousness is giving space for one's own inner guidance to come forward. This is illustrated by the prophecy in the Scriptures that a time would come when the voice of God would be heard directly by individuals without needing the intercession of a king or priest. It is this understanding of the much larger sphere of life that underlines everything that we teach at Garden Village. In the space of joy, loving care, and sense of well-being that we facilitate, people can more easily access Spirit and their own accurate inner guidance.

The interns have learned a lot, helped develop Garden Village physically, and added their youthful spirit, love, and excitement to our project. For the purpose of telling our story, I must use the clumsy tool of language that we have, but it pains me to call them "the interns" because they are so much more than that. They are my friends, my children, my teachers, my colleagues, my playmates! They are a living representation of unity and Oneness, yet each one is also special in my heart as an individual expression of love. They are not "they". They are me. We are One.

With these wonderful friends, I have also satiated my deep desire for loving the soil, planting, caring for and harvesting natural foods and then preparing beautiful, healthy, delicious meals with these gifts of the Mother. I love it ALL - the weeding, the composting, designing garden beds, incorporating flowers and other plants that attract bees and butterflies, and learning constantly from my indigenous friends in the area all that I can about this incredible, living world around me. Time disappears for me when I have my hands in the soil, especially when I'm with my friends, planting our first pineapple, teaching them how to harvest the yuca plant (SO delicious so many ways!), creating a corn field, or 100 other avenues to ecstasy.

We recognize that the Earth herself contains vast wisdom, and we are inspired to collaborate with her to merge our vision with hers. Day by day we seek to refine and deepen our relationship with her and together we dream of the day when all of man's ways will be in harmony with her.

In 2014, a young man brought turmeric to Garden Village as it was his favorite herb. I knew nothing about how to grow turmeric or if it was even suited for a tropical climate. I, however, honored his desire to find a place for it, and we lovingly planted it together. That young man left before ever seeing a single shoot, but I kept checking it and making sure it had sufficient water. After many weeks, two small shoots appeared, so I tenderly weeded around them. After two months, they were showing reasonable growth — right up until someone accidentally weed-whacked them and the experiment was sadly over. Or so I thought. One thing you learn in gardening — nature is persistent and strong and will have her way. Later that year, some new young folks came to be with us for awhile. They were installing trellises for beans and creating new garden beds when they came across a wonderful turmeric crop. They carefully expanded and marked that bed and now visitors enjoy turmeric with their Garden Village meals. I never serve it without thinking of that beautiful young man who brought it and left it as his gift to Garden Village. That is one story of so many that I could tell about these friends who lived on this land for a short time but will live in my heart forever.

There are many long days, intense heat, days of unrelenting rain, pesky mosquitoes and black gnats, difficult interactions with neighbors, seemingly limited funds, power outages and water main breaks to name some of the challenges — all part of the dream. Roses have thorns, you know, but a rose garden is still delightful. When those things arise, they provide a natural classroom affording us the opportunity to work together in a loving way with whatever the circumstance is. I won't claim that I never get tired or grumpy or worn down or even a bit depressed, but I LOVE where I am and wouldn't be anywhere else.

The vision of a place on earth where enlightened friends can dwell together in peaceful, purposeful living has indeed begun to manifest here. As we continue to expand, we want to do so in an easy, flowing way. When I first sense growth coming, I develop a vision of what might be the next natural place to be developed. Along with David, I go stand there for a while and simply see how it feels. When it doesn't seem to click, we leave that project and let it simmer. Some days I spend time just standing in the garden or pasture, leaning against a tree, or sitting on the ground with our dog in my lap just feeling rather than thinking. This pure communion with Life brings clarity of thought. When the timing is right, we feel it and begin to bring the next phase into form. How glorious it is for me to participate in this amazing, creative process. What once seemed impossible to me is now a reality.

PostScript

Susannah continues to live her dream. As of April 2016, over 35 interns had been to Garden Village along with many guests and relatives as visitors. A new greenhouse (Costa Rica jungle style) was erected by interns and some local help so that crops can be sheltered during the rainy season and increase their yield. The shower has been improved, increasing hot water capacity and privacy. Susannah has expanded her meadow-happy flock of hens to provide neighborhood eggs. Two smaller cabins and a larger cabin are under construction. An associate has purchased property next door, more than doubling the acreage at GardenVillage.

To learn more about Garden Village, see www.GardenVillageCosta Rica.org

Divine Nature Tours (DNT) continues to be a big part of Susannah's bliss. There was a DNT Retreat on the Pacific coast in January 2015 and another on the Caribbean side in February. Although these were not well-attended, those who came indicated that it was a remarkable experience in their lives. Two Retreats are planned for 2016. In addition to the regular tour in February, a special one is planned for March with Dr. Jon Mundy facilitating a Course In Miracles program. Susannah is excited about the possibility of working with other program leaders in a similar way for future Retreats.

Author's note: I began co-facilitating the Divine Nature Tour Retreats with Susannah in 2010 after having a life-altering experience myself on the Retreat. There have been two Retreats per year since then, and they always have a dramatic impact on the participants. I would invite you to join us. See details on www.DivineNatureTours.com.

INTRODUCTION TO "CALLED BY LOVE"

One way to discover your passion is to think about your skills. What are you good at? What comes easily to you? Follow this out and you will often come to the answer you've been seeking to the question, "What is the job I was created to do?"

If you're right, you may spend the rest of your life carrying on that work and all is well. But what if there is another aspect of life that is yours to do also? What if you have no background in that area? What if your skill set is perfect for it, but you have no idea what it is and seemingly no way to find your way to it? What if it is something that you would never think about, even in your wildest dreams? You'd never find it, right?

Well, Life has a way of leading you in the right direction if you just stay open to possibilities and say, "Come in", when opportunity knocks.

Meet Ed Bixby.....

CALLED BY LOVE

as told by Ed Bixby

Nobody was more surprised than I that I ended up owning and managing a cemetery. Even more surprising is how much I love it. As much as I enjoy building things through my construction company and giving back to the community through my charity work, nothing brings me the fulfillment that I find in empowering a family to feel like they have an active role in bringing peaceful closure to the life of a loved one and doing it in a way that enhances life rather than focuses on death. In fact, it was my own feeling that I needed to honor my deceased brother that led me to a life path that I wouldn't have found any other way.

To really understand how I got here, you have to go back more than 300 years. My ancestors, a family with thirteen children, moved to the US from Sweden in 1680 and acquired 195,000 acres outside of Atlantic City, NJ. This land stretched from Bakersfield (now Linwood) to Steelmantown. They created little villages throughout this tract that centered around activities that supported the industry of Steelmantown - a mill and mill pond for ship-building and making cedar shakes for roofs, cranberry bogs, and an ice house. The Cape Road, from Philadelphia to Cape May, ran through Steelmantown, so there was a thriving stagecoach inn there.

Where people live, people die. So my family created the Steelmantown Cemetery which was used as a burial ground from around 1700 up to 1840. At that time, they deeded the property to Upper Township to allow interment of dead from that area and to erect a schoolhouse and a house of worship. It continually served that purpose under the care of my family through 1957. When the first chapel burned down in a forest fire in the late 1800's, my great-grandfather built a second one. My grandmother taught Sunday school there and my mother attended that school. All things change and, in 1957, the township opted to auction off the burial grounds to Marvin Johnson, the local funeral director, for $35.

This was a very rural area in a simpler time. Up until 1950, there was no electricity in my mother's house. People did things the old ways. They would lay out their dead in their own homes and bury them by themselves in the cemetery. There were no rules regarding vaults or burial procedures. Marvin was called on mostly to bury wards of the State - forgotten people with no one to bury them. He did it as a service and charged only $10 per person to be buried in a simple pine box in an unmarked grave. The church congregation pretty much left by 1962 and the church building burned down in 1980, breaking the last link to my family. Marvin wasn't interested in maintaining the burial grounds so it fell into serious disrepair. The small chapel that my great-grandfather had built was vandalized and burned and the grounds turned into a dumping area.

My older brother, George, was the last person from our family to be buried in the old family plot behind the chapel. In 2007, my mother asked me to see if there was some way to clean up the area as it saddened her heart to see my brother's grave so desecrated. I went to see Marvin who agreed that it should be cleaned up. It had been weighing on his conscience, but he was 87 years old and didn't have the means to hire someone to do it. He was happy to sign the property over to me and was pleased that someone cared enough to clean it up. I didn't see any value in the property but took it on as a favor to my mom. Three months and twenty dump truck loads of debris and garbage later, my dad and I had it in good shape. Once again, it was a respectful and beautiful resting place for my brother. It didn't seem like anyone else in the area had any connection to the cemetery so I didn't expect that there would be any other visitors. For me, I felt it was a job well done and that would be the end of it.

The Birth of an Idea

One morning I was reading the Atlantic City Press at breakfast. A professor from Stockton University had written an article on the "new concept of natural burials." To be a "green cemetery" it had to be part of or adjacent to a state forest and have no history of practicing traditional burials. The similarity to my newly-acquired property caught my attention, but I knew that I didn't have the necessary space available to add any new plots according to Marvin's old hand-drawn survey. On a hunch, I hired a surveyor for $200 who discovered that the property I owned was one full acre — twice what Marvin had thought it was. That meant that I had room for 500 burial plots. I contacted the State of NJ to see if there was any money available to restore burial grounds. There was not, but I learned that I could take money from selling plots and put that into the required Preservation and Maintenance (P&M) fund. I still wasn't sure that this was anything that I wanted to do, but it seemed like the stars were aligning. I, therefore, contacted the Green Burial Council to see if the property could be certified as a Natural Burial Ground, meaning that no vaults or embalming process was permitted. To initiate a new Green Cemetery involves major challenges of meeting state and local guidelines, acquiring proper permits, and coming up with the funds to buy the land. All of that pales, however, compared to the Preservation and Maintenance fund requirements for those who are not a religious entity. To become a Certificate of Authority Cemetery (CAC), you must show a minimum of $250,000 in your P&M fund, and this money is ***untouchable.*** You are only allowed to use the interest to maintain your property. Combined with the initial outlay for the land, a new owner wouldn't live long enough to see a profit on his/her investment. Since 1971, there have only been six applications for new Certificate of Authority Cemeteries in the State of NJ and only half of those ever opened their doors.

As I said, the stars were aligning for me. My cemetery had been grandfathered as a CAC because of its longevity. I was, therefore, able to bypass all of the normal requirements and open for business even though I only had $1700 in my P&M fund. The whole process was incredibly smooth.

Actually, this didn't surprise me. I have always been a glass-half-full type of person. I had left home in 1989 at seventeen years of age and started my own business without a hiccup. Since then, I have started several successful businesses. They always seemed to go as smoothly as the experience I had entering into the cemetery business.

<u>Green Cemetery Concept</u>

Long before there were cemeteries with acres of manicured lawns and flowers and the high maintenance costs that go with that, people used to bury their own dead. In doing so, they brought the respect, love, and reverence to this process that it deserves. Each person handled the grief of the moment in his/her own, individual way. The life and history of a community could be celebrated in the natural beauty and surround of their burial grounds. Families would often picnic there, and it felt like their lost relatives were present in spirit with them.

Today, people have been so far removed from the process for so long, they don't understand what they're missing. Death and dying have become taboo topics. People often ask me if the main idea of a Green Cemetery is to be more ecologically sound. Certainly that is part of it. The stones used in my cemetery are simple and from the local region. They are placed in a way that they eventually simply blend back into the forest. The burial plots are covered with local foliage. With simple pine or wicker boxes or no box and no embalming, the body returns to the earth much faster and more naturally. The real magic, however, is the cathartic effect that envelops people as they become a participant rather than a spectator at the final laying to rest of their loved ones. They come to the cemetery, which is really a forest, and walk the forest trails to choose a site that feels good to them. If so desired, they carry the body to the site, help lower it into the grave, and participate in filling in the dirt and placing the foliage and any flowers they brought on top. On return visits, they have the use of hiking/biking trails that interweave from our property into the adjacent Belleplain State Forest. This is a place for the living, not for the dead. With the natural beauty of the forest and the singing of the birds, people come back to celebrate life with their families and feel the Spirit of their departed ones just as it was done 150 years ago.

The Start-Up

You would think that step one would be to get some training in my new field of endeavor. I'm sure most people would have approached it that way. I, however, had learned to trust my instincts, so I launched the business with no training whatsoever.

When I sold my first plot, I really had no idea what I was doing. I simply prepared the grave in the way that felt good to me. Rather than bring in a backhoe, we dug the grave by hand and cut cedar boughs to place there. The family carried their loved one to the grave and, at the end of their own ceremony, began the process of filling the grave. I saw how meaningful it was to them and how it empowered them. I watched tears stream down the face of one of my gravediggers even though he had never met this family. Afterwards, the family came to me and expressed their gratitude for what we had done. It all clicked for me in that moment. I felt the passion rise in me to help other families in this way. I always believed that things happen for a reason and now I realized that this path had chosen me. I love helping people in one of the most challenging times of their lives. I was grateful that I was financially supported by my contracting business as I knew that I would be doing this new endeavor as a labor of love, not for much financial gain.

So I was now in business as a cemeterian. Having grown up in the area, I had a feeling for the natural surroundings. When I looked at the open field that people saw when they first came in, it seemed as though something was missing. Then it clicked - what was missing was the old chapel, so I re-created it as closely as I could to the original. As a real estate developer and land use planner, it was easy for me to survey the plots and design the trails through the forest myself. As a developer and builder, I knew how to run a business and already had two men on my payroll who dug footings for me. Digging graves isn't that much different. My dad did the property maintenance, and I met with all clients personally. It helped a lot that my wife, Kristin, was an attorney. She supported me by researching all of the NJ rules and regulations as well as liability issues to make sure that I handled my responsibilities properly.

Once I got started, the passion filled me. I found that I really enjoyed meeting with families and showing them how this could be a different experience from the usual funeral. This was something unique that I believed in deeply as I saw how it benefitted the individual plot owners. Each interaction was different and memorable both for me and for the families. I can still picture each person with whom I had visited clearly in my mind and remember their names. I also could see how this was becoming a gift to the community, much as my family had originally intended those many years ago. So I was thrilled when the opportunity arose to purchase an adjacent property, expanding the cemetery to ten acres. We were literally changing the face of funeral arrangements in New Jersey. Now I felt like I wanted to do more.

Expanding the Vision

The first modern Natural Burial Ground was started in England in 1995. Now there are over 250 there and more than 50% of burials in England are natural. In the US, it is a mere fraction of the market; and I wanted to see more people exposed to this alternative throughout the country. I want to re-introduce American society to the ways of our past and demystify the funeral director and local cemetery by making them an integral part of community life. Though I've never been a public speaker, I felt compelled to teach other cemeterians about this option and guide them in offering it to the public. This opportunity wasn't long in coming.

Joe Sehee, founder of the Green Burial Council (GBC), came to visit and told me that I had the best natural cemetery in the U.S. even though I had just laid it out according to what felt right to me. More than 20 of the biggest cemetery landscape architects in the country contacted me in my first seven years in the business to ask me for my plan. They were astounded when I told them I had no plan! I became active in the GBC. I was soon asked to give talks to owners of small cemeteries about taking this approach and to owners of large cemeteries about dedicating a small portion of their land to natural burial. I introduce them to the concept of making their cemetery a vital part of their community. I share that I had open houses and invited groups of school children out to enjoy the beauty of the place which gave them a new impression of burial grounds. They see how much life and community history is present in their local cemetery. I don't consider myself an expert or a polished speaker, yet I'm asked to speak at conventions. People believe in what I have to share because they can feel my passion and commitment.

Natural burial is not a fad. As people come to understand it, they will see how empowering and healing it is for the family. More people will want this alternative and, like in England, it will become more of a part of the mainstream. As the demand increases, the funeral industry will come to embrace this as a viable option and expand the availability of Green Cemeteries in partnership with the traditional approach. As this comes to pass and an increasing number of people come to find an experience of expanded life after death, my passion will have been realized.

Postscript

Ed Bixby has now been fully embraced by the cemetery industry even though he is a relative new-comer with no formal training. He is now President of the Green Burial Council and sits on its International Board focusing heavily on educational programs for funeral directors, as well as the public. He continues to give presentations for the National Funeral Directors' Association, GBC, and International Cemetery, Cremation, and Funeral Association, as well as many smaller regional and local associations.

When Ed opened his cemetery, he was one of only about a dozen certified National Burial Grounds in the U.S. In 2015, that number was up to twenty-two. Within ten years, Ed hopes that twenty percent of burials in the U.S. will be green burials.

He also has a vision of taking historic cemeteries and turning them over to the Audubon Society, Sierra Club, or similar non-profit organizations, which could build their P&M funds via donations. Even old, badly maintained cemeteries from the 1700s and 1800s could blend into local communities by creating butterfly gardens, wildflower prairies or simply cared-for areas where local events could be held.

In addition to his broader work, he still manages Steelmantown Cemetery Green Burial Preserve. He chooses to put 30% of all income into his Preservation and Maintenance Fund rather than the required 15%. As the only natural burial grounds in New Jersey, 90% of his business comes from New Jersey and New York. He has, however, had people come from as far as California to have loved ones buried there. As busy as he is with his construction business, charity work, and being the public face for the natural burial movement, Ed loves working in his cemetery and talking with new families all the time.

When I asked him why it excites him so, he told me the story of the cemetery stone in front of the restored chapel. It simply reads, "Oxley". That family now lives in Margate, about 25 miles away. The family read about an open house at the old cemetery. They hadn't visited in over twenty years and came out of curiosity. The current patriarch of the family was 90 years old and his grandparents were buried there. He couldn't believe how beautiful the grounds looked. "I feel like it's 1940 again, seeing my grandparents resting place and that beautiful little chapel right where it always was. I never thought I'd see this scene again," he said as he made a donation to the P&M fund. That's the reward for which Ed lives.

Rather than more work, he sees it as his release and fulfillment in life. He wants to pass this business on to his children, and he believes that they will have the same passion for it that he does.

INTRODUCTION TO "THE WHITE LION LADY OF TIMBAVATI"

Money? Check.

Success? Check.

Exciting life? Check.

Health? Check.

Beauty? Check.

Marriage and family? Check.

Satisfying career? Check.

So why would anyone walk away from all of that to spend years in the jungle with little, if any, pay? Why would someone swim upstream by trying to buck the accepted scientific community? Why would someone risk her life and future and expose herself to potential ridicule?

Most people wouldn't. One person did. Meet Linda Tucker.........................

THE WHITE LION LADY
OF TIMBAVATI

To see a White Lion is to know awe. Mythical is the word that came to my mind the first time I ever saw one. I was mesmerized by the beauty, gracefulness, and power embodied in this ghost-like regal beast in front of me.

Sadly, if you have ever seen one of these amazing animals it was probably in a zoo or a circus as they have been *entirely* eliminated in the wild by hunters seeking them as trophies or for captivity and only 13 currently exist in a protected area of their natural habitat. The fact that *any* live outside of cages is due to the efforts of The Global White Lion Protection Trust (GWLPT), a non-profit, community-based conservation organization dedicated to the preservation of the White Lions and the education of humankind as to the significance of this unique creature. This is the story behind the story.

The White Lion Lady

Linda Tucker has a purpose beyond ensuring the survival of the White Lions. She wants to help humanity discover lion-leadership – the quality of fearlessness inspired through love and reverence for nature that has the capability of changing the world. She says that we can only discover this by reawakening to our hearts. That is the path to empowerment to solve the crises we have created as a "cold-hearted" species.

Linda believes that following your bliss, finding your passion and acting on what you were born to do is the way to reawaken your heart and connect you to the fearlessness of lion-leadership. To discover that for herself, it meant leaving the world of the 9-5 corporate existence that is the foundation of consumer society, moving to Africa and founding the GWLPT and the White Lion Leadership Academy. As you might guess, it is not lions that attend the Academy but rather people who come to be inspired by the great heart of the White Lions so that they can tap into their own fearlessness and pursue what is theirs to do.

Discovering this unusual calling involved a story with some twists and turns, just like all of our lives, but it started with an experience far more dramatic than most people ever have.

Meeting the Lion Queen

Born in South Africa, Linda was exposed to the legend of the White Lions as a child when she visited Timbavati where they were reported to live. Timbavati takes its name from the local Shangaan language, translated as "the place where the lions came down from the stars." Fascinated by the legend, she was disappointed not to actually see these regal animals.

While in South Africa she began her study of psychology and medieval symbolism at the University of Cape Town. She left for England and finished her degree at Cambridge in England. Her career took a left turn when she became a fashion model for Yardley and L'Oreal in the UK and later a fashion advertising executive for an international company. Some might find that part of her story interesting but she says that her "real life" began with a vacation with friends back in the region of her birth.

On November 10 of 1991, she was on safari holiday with her husband, her sister, and a few friends on the edge of South Africa's Kruger National Park when they heard that a lioness was due to give birth in the wild, possibly to a white cub. Excited by the possibility of encountering the mythical beast she had so longed to see as a child, they borrowed a

WWII-type open jeep and set out for the area where this lioness was reported to be. They later discovered that they had indeed approached a riverbed in which a golden lioness had just birthed a white lion cub. A more immediate concern, however, was that they got hung up with a broken steering shaft on a tree stump in the midst of a pride of 24 lions with night quickly approaching. Worse yet, they had no cell phone or radio contact. Panic gripped them all.

When people panic, they emit the smell of fear, exactly like prey. When people act like prey, predators act like predators. The lions surrounded them and began to close their circle. The cats were hidden by the moonless night which had now enveloped them in its inky blackness. Their only protection was the light from a small spotlight. Hearing rustling to their left, they shone the spotlight there revealing a lioness less than 10 meters away in a predatory crouch. She backed off but then a similar rustling came from the other side. Spinning the spotlight in that direction revealed a huge male in attack mode. His bright amber eyes were gleaming and sharply focused. His frightening teeth menacingly bared. Recalling stories of a lion with a lost tail, like this one, they knew that this was the lion called Thor – a very aggressive male who was known to charge vehicles. It's not hard to imagine the intense fear that filled each one of them.

The battery to which their spotlight was connected was losing power. Most members of the group were now screaming and waving their arms in sheer terror. This behavior incites predators so they become even more dangerous. Basically, they were providing the lions an open and inviting butcher shop where they were the meat. With no commercial camps anywhere near them, they absolutely knew that one or more of them would be eaten alive, and there was no way out.

Into this nightmare, through the pitch darkness and right through the pride of 24 angry lions walked a regal looking woman with a baby on her back and a small girl and boy following close behind. She carried no light or weapon – just an invisible flaming torch of courage. She climbed right into the jeep and seemed to pass that flame on to one of the men. A man who had moments ago been just as deeply panicked as everyone, now calmly said, "You all stay here. I'll take the wheel spanner and walk through the lions to go get help." The woman told him to go with the young boy she had come with, and he would be safe. Somehow, all in the jeep felt peaceful and assured, and even the lion pride had calmed down. Along with the boy, he walked straight through them without incident, returning in about 45 minutes in a Land Rover, saving the entire party. Of course, the true hero of that night was that incredible woman whom they later discovered was a powerful shaman from a royal family – a sangoma, a shamanic healer who advised Kings and Queens as a messenger of the Divine. This woman was known as The Lion Queen of Timbavati. Linda knew none of that at the time, and she certainly had no clue as to the huge impact this woman was to have on her future.

The Awakening

Returning to her life as a corporate executive in London, Paris, and other parts of Europe, she felt a shift inside of herself that negated the value of that existence. Life was empty and hollow. When she told the story of her African experience at dinner parties, she knew that there was something far more significant than an adventure to be recounted. It became clear that she had been unhappy for many years, and now the insane artificiality of her world was apparent. It was a powerful world of controlling minds through branding and marketing; but with the perspective of her dramatic experience in South Africa, she now saw it as totally meaningless. The Lion Queen, a woman she later came to know as Maria Khosa, had lit a fire deep within her. Even so, she wasn't yet prepared to acknowledge and honor that flame. There was a huge internal resistance to following the Truth she felt stirring in her soul. Fear was separating her from her true path in life. Her husband, a Cambridge academic, fueled the resistance and reminded her of the advantages that she had as a high-flying executive who had always lived the "privileged" life.

Yet this spark that had been ignited within was not to be denied. She couldn't sleep for six weeks. She hardly ate anything at all. She could barely function. The fire of Truth that had been lit continued to grow until, in a few years, it totally consumed the fear and resistance. Linda could no longer live a lie. It took a total breakdown in her glamorous life to break through to the true meaning of Life. She later realized that it was the lion heart in her that activated the love that enabled her to overcome the fear. In

1994, Linda Tucker turned her back on her highly-regarded career, home, husband, and all that was familiar to return to her birthplace and track down this woman who had connected her to the raw, godly creation that is lions in the wilderness. She needed an answer to the question that had been consuming her consciousness for three years, "How could a woman walk through lions with a baby on her back and two little ones behind her and face death so calmly?"

Discovering Her Passion

It was not difficult finding Maria in her traditional village. She looked up and said to Linda, "What took you so long to wake up?" She responded to Linda's burning question, with an almost scornful laugh, and offered her explanation. "There was no danger. Would a grandmother take her babies into the jaws of death? Lions are my family. They are Lions of God. Having the children with me was my show of faith". When reminded of how aggressive the lions were acting and how imminent an attack appeared, she gave that scornful laugh again, looked at Linda with patience in her eyes like someone would look at a small child asking silly questions and said, "Don't you realize that YOU were the aggressors. You drove into sacred space where a lioness was giving birth to a rare and sacred white lion cub. You were the ones making noise and flailing about, disturbing the sanctity of that place and that event. The lions were merely protectors of the white lion cub born that night. This was a most special and sacred event as the last white cub had been born into the sacred lands of origin and was subsequently stolen by humans. For two decades since that time, the White Lion in the wild was virtually extinct due to hunting and captures for zoos and circuses. They were caged and shot while helpless just for trophies and you wonder why they were aggressive that night when you threatened this new, precious cub."

Linda was hooked. Suddenly, the meaning of her studies of ancient symbolism and literature at Cambridge University clicked into place. It had been predicted that this time was to be a tipping point, a time of great change. It was foretold that this would be a time where Man was required to cooperate with Nature who would be restoring herself, with or without us. The Earth – Gaia – is ready to work with those who are open to restoring their proper contract with nature – to accept their rightful position as stewards, not rapists, of the Earth. Maria had known three years ago that this knowledge was known deep inside of Linda. It took all of that time, however, for Linda to escape the story that had been ingrained in her consciousness – the conviction that the life of material wealth was reality. Linda had been trapped in unsustainable cages of consumerism, a bad marriage, a glamorous but unfulfilling career, societal expectations, and false realities. Hearing about the White Lions being trapped in horrible cages woke her up and let her see her own cages. She was inspired to break free and to accept her true lion-hearted Nature. It was clear that the aberrant human behavior that she witnessed on the planet was due to leaving our natural roots and connection to Nature, with which we are naturally co-creators. Linda now understands that the White Lions are here to invite us to reclaim our true contract with Nature – not as primitive innocents but as a mature species ready to overcome the errors of our past ways. Linda saw that she had a key role to play in this outworking.

Maria Khosa may have been seen by white South Africans as a lowly black domestic worker without any significance; yet people who knew the truth of her Spirit would walk miles to be healed by this revered Tsonga medicine woman. Though she had little money herself, she never charged anything for her services as she considered her service as a Divine gift to be shared freely. In her tribal culture, she held the highest position and commanded the greatest respect. Linda felt the radiant power of this woman. It was easy to accept that she had a special relationship with the lions and a vital mission to realize on earth. Linda's part to play in all this was less clear and she didn't know what would be expected of her. She also didn't understand her relationship to Maria.

Maria remained patient and gentle as she explained that Linda was her daughter and her successor as the Keeper of the White Lions, an ancient Shamanic title. Head spinning, Linda asked how she could be her daughter when one was white and the other black. That brought forth another wonderful Maria laugh as she said, "In the higher Reality, you are my 'star-daughter', beyond color and race. You and I are lionesses. We rub cheeks in greeting. You rub your black cheek with me, your ancestry, but show your white cheek to the world. In this way, you are a bridge to the modern world so they can understand our ancient knowledge to advance lion tradition."

The quality of lion-heartedness is fearlessness driven by Love. Recognizing that this was what brought Linda to Maria, she knew that it was time to stop counting costs and risks. She just had to move boldly ahead to protect these Divine creatures doing whatever was required. It was in this way that she could help the lions complete their mission to help Humanity in the transformation necessary at this time in history. Thus, the daughter came back to her mother to learn from this powerful shamanic teacher.

The Value of Her Early Life

Linda Tucker was in a unique position to validate the authenticity of the ancient knowledge in a modern context. Though she might have seen her prior experience as unrelated, it had prepared her for this, her true work. The skills, connections and financial acumen developed in the corporate world were critical to her ability to found the Global White Lion Protection Trust in 2002. The goal of the GWLPT was to return White Lions to the wild. Her background in marketing, branding, social media and understanding mass media enabled her to co-create fund-raising and promotional events and provided the necessary savvy to handle the negative press. This bad press came, not only from the people you might expect, but also from competitive conservation groups! The first few years of her work were supported by money she had earned as a fashion model and executive as well as from contributions from very generous friends made during those years. These are just some of the elements that made up the "white cheek" that Maria knew would be important.

Linda's studies at Cambridge, a center for modern knowledge, was another important aspect of her past. This experience helped her to develop an analytical mind critical to the intensive research necessary to understand more about the legends and myths regarding the White Lions and to uncover the verifiable facts on which they were based. Combining the great depth of the indigenous knowledge systems that Maria represented with university studies of medieval symbolism, Linda discovered, to her astonishment, that the White Lions' sacred lands, where the Star Lions first appeared, aligned exactly with Giza. This was where the Great Sphinx, mankind's greatest lion riddle, is located. How can this be unrelated to the Divine workings of the Cosmos? In fact, Shamanic elders describe the White Lion as the first born of God's creatures and say that there was a White Lion on either side of the Throne of God.

She now saw clearly that her earlier life, far from being meaningless, had been exactly what was required to put her in position to fulfill her true mission in Life.

The Mission and the Birth of Marah

Maria Khosa knew a simple truth from the ancient knowledge: when we show love and respect to Nature, it responds in kind. That fateful day when she walked through that lion pride, she knew that there was no chance of her or the children being harmed by the lions as long as she had nothing but love and respect in her heart and in her actions towards them. That law is as fundamentally true as the law of gravity so there were no doubts in her mind. It was from this that Linda developed the two principles on which the Global White Lion Protection Trust was founded:

1. Show Nature Love and respect and you will never be harmed
2. Nature will return only Love and respect

The GWLPT is a scientific, non-profit organization that combines indigenous knowledge with scientific research. One of their goals is to prove that the White Lion is a unique species so they can be listed as endangered. One would think this would be obvious since, though there are hundreds of them in zoos and circuses around the world, at the time of the writing of this book only 13 live in wild habitat. Tragically, it is still legal to hunt them. Being rare, they have become greatly sought after as the highest income trophies. Those with such an agenda have been very active for years disseminating misinformation. They claim that White Lions are freaks with no conservation value who are unable to hunt or camouflage themselves in the wild due to their white color. Even though this has been proven false, people hear only what they want to believe if it serves their agenda. As an offspring of the golden lions, they are not albino, as many believe, but rather the result of a recessive gene that inhibits the pigment in their fur while also giving them striking blue eyes. The GWLPT has now been working for ten years with scientists in seven countries (U.S., U.K., Canada, China, Korea, Nimibia, and South Africa) doing intensive genetic research comparing the genetic code of the White Lion with the Snow Leopard, Tiger, Kimodo Bear, and small cats. They were searching for the unique element that makes them a separate species from the golden lions. One would have better odds of finding a needle in a haystack. Yet, in 2013, the BBC announced that they had indeed discovered the genetic marker that makes White Lions unique. The GWLPT has now started the arduous process of getting the White Lion protected by international law. With so few White Lions alive in the wild, it is a race against time, moving through the bureaucratic maze of this process.

The birth of that White Lion cub in 1991 not only changed Linda's life forever, but it also enabled Maria to identify the specific male golden lion that carried the genetic code of the White Lion. He was to be the forefather of future generations. Maria also identified him as Linda's guardian lion. Unfortunately, that lion was also identified by hunters as the next great trophy. Maria and Linda did their best to disseminate the information that this regal beast was considered a holy entity by the indigenous people, but that was not enough to dissuade the hunters; and they could not be stopped from hunting him down. They killed him on the sacred day when the Sun crosses the heart star (Regulus) of the Leo constellation. This day was known by ancient Egypt as the holiest day of the year – a day when a King returns to his Kingdom in the stars or a King or Queen is born on earth. Maria saw this as no coincidence. Linda's respect and reverence for the indigenous knowledge system that she upheld deepened with the recognition that Nature is sacred and, as Maria put it, White Lions are indeed "Lions of God". Her years of studying astrology enabled Linda to understand this event more clearly and see why these amazing Beings should be called Star Beasts. There is an extraordinary connection between White Lions and a star plan taking place on earth. The White Lions are believed to be bearers of enlightenment, here to restore natural order to the ecosystem and cosmic order on Earth. (For more information about the White Lions, read Linda's book, *Mystery of the White Lions: Children of the Sun God* and see her website: www.WhiteLions.org).

Following the death of Linda's guardian lion, known as Ingwavuma, she was afraid that was the end of the line, that the last gene-bearer was gone. Life, however, had a greater plan. Because Ingwavuma had been the Lion King governing this region for several years, he had been mating within several prides. After three generations, the genetic code began appearing again in the wild. Amazingly, this timing coincided perfectly with the scientific efforts being made by the Global White Lion Protection Trust to remove White Lions from captivity and return them to the wild. Three prides of White Lions were restored to the wilderness by the GWLPT, integrating them with the golden lions in the way they normally occur. These efforts began to restore the natural balance.

Marah was the first White Lion returned to the wild. Maria Khosa had predicted that the Queen of the White Lions would be born in a place and on a date considered holy by people of the Western world. On Christmas morning in the year 2000, a ball of white fur was born in the small African village of Bethlehem. This was the cub that came to be known as Marah (meaning mother of Rah, the sun god) - named by African elders who told Linda that Marah was "The One" they had been waiting for. Yet this seemed impossible as the lion cub was born in a hunting camp destined for an early and brutal death.

This awareness burned in Linda's consciousness and dictated her actions from that moment on. She knew that it was her mission to rescue Marah from this camp and return her to the wild where she would become Queen of the new generations of White Lions. Her battle to free Marah and her siblings is recounted in Linda's book, *Saving the White Lions: One Woman's Battle for Africa's Most Sacred Animal*. For purposes of this story, it suffices to say that Marah was successfully rescued and released into her rightful Kingdom in a 4400 acre protected area of endemic bushveld. There, she proved wrong those who claimed that, due to their color hindering their ability to hunt successfully, White Lions could not survive in the wild. To the contrary, Marah bore and raised three cubs (Regeus, Zihra, and Letaba) in the wild and successfully taught them to hunt and be as self-sufficient as their tawny cousins. After seven years of reigning over her pride and insuring the propagation of White Lions in the wild, Marah died free, remarkably on Easter day.

The Meaning

I would like to end this story with Linda's own words.

"The passion that I have for this work is the greatest love I could ever experience – a lioness mother's unconditional and fearless love to overcome any and all challenges. It is this timeless love that drives me, and I am so grateful to have found this deep meaning for my life. A lot of this work is brutally challenging: hunters, red tape, delays, lack of understanding, and, of course, death – death of these noble Beings at the hands of hunters; and, most crushing to me, the death of my star-mother, Maria Khosa, in 2010. Amazingly, Maria transitioned on the very day that the book I dedicated to her was published. I still feel her guiding my process and sending me signs; and so, I remain unerringly committed to this work. How could I not? Indigenous priests of many tribes recognize the White Lion as the most sacred animal on the continent – prophetic legendary animals – King of Kings – light bearers carrying a Divine message to activate Lion-Hearted leadership in humanity and awaken us to the true responsibility of stewardship of the Earth. In the ancient sacred texts of Egypt, White Lions are seen as guardians of the Human Soul and connected with dolphins and whales as a key to saving Humanity.

I have witnessed the worst of humanity and still know that there is hope for us. My mission might be seen as daunting, but I never question it. I know that Love is the greatest force in the Universe and cannot be defeated. My work is not *for* the White Lions but rather *with* the White Lions to bring about a quantum shift in human consciousness. This shift is critical at this time in history for Mankind to rediscover right relationship with Nature and realize true Oneness once again."

Postscript

The purpose of this book is to show how people discovered and followed their bliss in life. It is not meant to tell their entire story. Linda Tucker's story is phenomenal, as is her mission. Both deserve far more consideration than the scope of this story gives them. If you have been touched by this small look into her life, then I recommend reading her books, *Mystery of the White Lions: Children of the Sun God* and *Saving the White Lions: One Woman's Battle for Africa's Most Sacred Animal.* Both are available on Amazon in written and e-book formats.

It should be noted that Linda's amazing work through the Global White Lion Protection Trust is far from over. As of the writing of this book, White Lions are still not registered as an endangered species, hunting them is still legal, and they are highly sought-after trophies. Their ancestral lands are being carved up for agricultural and other uses, leaving them in further peril. To find out how you can help, go to <u>WhiteLions.org</u>.

INTRODUCTION TO "THE CHANGING FACE OF BLISS"

Sometimes, Bliss morphs.

Perhaps it comes to you at an early age in a flash of enlightenment while watching a TV special. That vision stays with you and forms your early life through school. It even determines your first career. That passion burning inside of you helps develop the principles that become the foundation of your life. You move ahead, confident in your direction and knowing that you are firmly in touch with your Life's purpose. Right up until you collide head-on with a wall of disillusionment. How wonderful to have your world rocked and dissolved! Now you are free to release your Gibralter-like constructs and discover what your life is REALLY about! Meet Andrew Horwood................

THE CHANGING
FACE OF BLISS

There is a place near Gawler in South Australia called Riverdell Spiritual Centre. Visit there and you will immediately notice something different – something magical that permeates the air. You may not be able to put your finger on it but you will feel a peace and ease that is unmistakable.

Who is this white-haired man striding towards you with his 1000-watt smile and eyes that warm your soul? Why do you feel so comfortable in his presence? You take his outstretched hand as he welcomes you to his home and you know that you've just made a friend for life. Andrew Horwood is the Program Director for Riverdell but that is only a title. In truth, he is a man whose passion is for each person to discover and express the greatness they hold within themselves and it is that invitation that you feel.

Ask Andrew and he will tell you that there is no place he would rather be and nothing he would rather be doing. It's certainly not for the money and there are few material perks, but freeing people into a greater experience of Love has been his passion since he saw the wide, sad eyes of starving children in India looking deep into his heart from a movie screen. He heard a calling – a Divine invitation to purpose. He was all of twelve years old on that day. He didn't fully understand what had just happened to him. He only knew, in the core of his Being where mental processes don't interfere, that the course of his life had just been established. His left brain translated that for him as a desire to become a U.N. doctor who would travel to India and save those children.

Australia is not India and the people who visit Riverdell are not starving Indian children, yet Andrew is living his dream every day of his life. So let's take a look at the winding road that connects those dots.

The Beginning

Andrew was one of four children born to academic parents with socialist leanings who agreed with Karl Marx that religion was the opium of the masses, designed to control people who didn't think for themselves. At that time, he was firmly resistant to the possibility that Spirit might play a constructive role in a person's life. Yet while he accepted that, he still had an intense desire to help people find a freedom and a sense of joy in living and in relationships that he didn't see in his own family. Through high school and university, he held on to a belief that he could achieve this goal via the scientific, medical model since he eschewed the religious approach. Intuitively, he felt that, if he could help people achieve a state of robust physical health, they would find their way to happiness.

Somewhere in medical school, the vision of being a U.N. doctor helping Indian children morphed into the picture of a general practitioner helping the people of Australia find this freedom. At this point, he was still confident that medicine had the power to make a lasting difference in people's lives beyond physical well-being. As a doctor, he was going to help people find a greater experience of love in their lives. He had studied basic psychology and was sure that he could boost people to the higher levels of Maslow's pyramid to find inner fulfillment. In spite of, or perhaps because of, the fact that he never experienced this total fulfillment in his own family, he developed a bullet-proof optimism and conviction that he could author this experience for others. That was his theory.

There's no better way to test what you know than through personal experience. In 1972, full of optimism and midway through medical training, Andrew thought he could help a schizophrenic acquaintance through her psychosis on his own. He says "I was way out of my depth", and as a result, became burned out and severely depressed. He recalls driving a car and not being able to look left or right as it took so long that he wouldn't be able to tell if the road ahead was changing. He saw a psychiatrist and was given medication, but chose instead to take time off from medical school and hitchhike across Australia. When he came back 3 months later, his girlfriend was gone and his life seemed to be falling apart.

Yet the following year marked a new beginning. He resumed medical school. He changed houses where a few months later, Lyell, his life-partner-to-be, moved in. Recognizing a need for skill as well as optimism, he trained with Lifeline, a telephone crisis counseling service, meeting inspiring trainers who helped broaden his understanding of helping others. These two years were in essence a "death and resurrection" experience. And more was to come.

Early in 1974, 25 year-old Andrew was in his next-to-last year of medical school in Melbourne. One day, his father, Keith, had lunch with him, as he often did. This time, Andrew saw a depth of despair in his father; and, for the first time as an adult, he said, "I love you Dad." The simple reply was, "That's nice" as they walked together in a new state of intimacy back to the University. It was the only time he could remember letting the full depth of love inside him flow freely to his father. Those 30 seconds impacted him greatly.

Within weeks, his father left for England on study leave. A few months later, Keith died suddenly of a heart attack. When Andrew got the call from his mother, he felt both intense heartache and an overwhelming sense of gratitude for having shared those last precious moments with his father. It was so significant for him that it birthed a future practice of encouraging his dying patients to speak or write their deepest feelings to their loved ones. There is nothing quite like impending death to bring focus to your highest truth.

Recognizing the impact of connecting with his father through love fueled the fire, opened his understanding of the power of healing the emotional heart. During his five years of post–graduate medical training he was inspired by doctors with great integrity and deep caring for their patients. He also saw doctors lacking those traits. Mastering this body of intellectual knowledge was very satisfying to the young doctor-to-be and he felt strongly that these technical skills combined with his optimism and personal experiences would be critical to realizing his vision. "When I get to the starting line, I'll do it my way and have great impact on many lives," he thought.

In 1981, at age 32, Dr. Andrew Horwood hung out his shingle with the Lister House Clinic in the country town of Horsham, Victoria, Australia as a general medical practitioner. This was living his bliss: being with the woman he loved, living in a beautiful country environment, and finally in place to fulfill the vision he had had since he was twelve years old.

Disillusionment and Beginning of Enlightenment

One of the first patients for whom he prescribed a new anti-inflammatory medication was a 75 year-old woman suffering from osteoarthritis. This "miracle" drug was touted as putting an end to exactly that type of pain. Instead, the patient almost died from a bleeding peptic ulcer caused by the drug. Several similar incidents with various drugs over the next few years made him look carefully at the well-intentioned actions he was taking and the anomalous results. Even when his medical skills achieved positive results by improving the physical health of the patients, it was rare that they would move up Maslow's pyramid to the inner fulfillment that Andrew wished for them. Something was surely missing.

An early clue as to what this missing component might be came to him within weeks of starting his practice in Horsham. A farmer in his sixties came to see him. It quickly became clear he had late stage lung cancer. Medical specialists at the time could offer him nothing curative, so he sought help from a healer. Using energy healing techniques, this woman said his cancer was curable, allowing him to live with strong hope. Andrew provided medical support as needed and his relationship with this man and his wife deepened as they journeyed together. Within 6 months it was clear this man was dying. Andrew asked him if there was anything he'd like to happen before he died and he said, "I'd like to take communion". A devout Catholic who had divorced his first wife, this farmer had remarried and had not been welcome to share communion ever since, as his marriage was not recognized by the Church. Andrew contacted the wise Catholic priest in Horsham who arranged both a Church marriage ceremony and communion. Three days later, this farmer died a happy man. Love had found a way to triumph through all these difficulties that the farmer faced. And medicine had played a very small part.

Andrew liked to push the boundaries of medical practice. In his quest to find peers, he became a Medical Educator for the Family Medicine Program of the Royal Australian College of General Practitioners. This group of educator-doctors, while in mainstream medicine, were likewise interested in the leading edge of medical practice and Andrew found colleagues here with whom he could share the longing of his heart for holistic medicine.

Yes, he was helping people and he could even see significant changes in the lives of some of his patients; but the grand dream wasn't appearing – the reality was a pale imitation of the powerful dream he held. He had reached the pinnacle of his quest to be a doctor and discovered that it was far less satisfying than he had anticipated. The medical model he had embraced was not only inadequate; it was, in significant ways, counter-productive. As he had been taught, he accepted the solutions prescribed by pharmaceutical companies which presented them as though the doctor would be almost unethical not to prescribe them.

Development of Spiritual Awareness

Andrew's resistance to spirituality had been softening for some time. While living in Melbourne, Lyell had suggested that they attend St Michael's Uniting Church where Dr Francis Macnab was minister. Combining ministry and psychology, he intrigued Andrew by the way he blended these in a way that made sense to him. By now he knew that to do any true healing he would have to address the psychology as well as the physicality of his patients. He also recognized Dr. Macnab as a strong person who knew a different spirituality – certainly not someone who fit the sheep-like caricature his parents had painted of "God-fearing people". Andrew became more aware of the possibility that spirituality might have a place in his life after all.

Lyell Gough and Andrew Horwood had taken their marriage vows on June 14th, 1975 in the Uniting Church in Branxholme, Victoria, a small country township close to where Lyell had grown up. Her parents and grandparents had married at that Church. It was not particularly significant to Andrew to be married in a church but he agreed to Lyell's wishes

During the 1980s, a number of pivotal influences helped shape Andrew's awareness and consciousness. On September 29th, 1982, that consciousness opened as though someone had exploded a dam wall releasing the flood waters of truth into his mind. The trigger was the entrance into the world of Samuel James Horwood, Andrew and Lyell's first child. As Andrew beheld the miracle of his son, it occurred to him how little he had contributed to the birth of this extraordinary new Being. Even though he had delivered many babies and felt humbled at the presence of new life, holding his own new-born son brought the revelation that there was some other benevolent force outside of his will and mental abilities that had given him this remarkable gift. His life passed across his mental screen in a way he had never viewed it before. He now saw invisible guidance having a hand in events to which he had previously given no thought: the "coincidence" of he and Lyell moving into the same student housing; going to Horsham as a first-year intern, loving it, and having a GP position open up there five years later, just as he was ready to commence practice; going to the Uniting Church in Melbourne to hear Dr Francis Macnab without knowing what an impact he would later have on Andrew's life.

Just holding his baby brought recognition that these were not chance events but that there was some design at work and it was acting for his good. Overcoming his early convictions about the absence of God, he now recognized this benevolent force at a deep level and realized that it must be operating in everyone's life. This was the missing element that his vaunted medical model did not speak to.

The power of this mystical revelation he had at the birth of his son led him to join the Uniting Church in Horsham where he and Lyell became active participants, developing deep friendships with the ministers there.

Andrew felt within him an urge to keep looking for a vision and practice of medicine that matched his intuitive knowing of what was possible. This led him to explore widely and push the boundaries of what was accepted in medicine at the time. He knew now that there was something larger than science, yet still felt that his medical skills could play a part in his mission to raise people up into a consciousness of love.

In 1984, he attended a Wellness Day event and was mesmerized by one of the presenters, Dr. Richard Hetzel, who was a holistic G.P. and president of the Whole Health Institute (WHI) in Australia. Andrew was instantly drawn to his philosophy. He learned that in 1949, the World Health Organization had defined health as "a state of complete physical, mental and social well-being and not merely the absence of disease or infirmity." This fueled his vision for wholeness as the goal for his medical work.

Through Richard Hetzel, Andrew met practitioners of many disciplines who shared his vision. He became active in WHI, hosting regular meetings in his home in Horsham for several years from the late 80s to promote that vision.

Reviewing the history of medical practice, Andrew realized that most innovations in care had arisen from clinicians at the coalface making observations about their patients and trying new things. This was in contrast to recent decades when practice relied upon evidence-based medicine and changes weren't recommended until years of therapeutic trials, which can slow down the process of innovation. This realization encouraged Andrew to be curious about and keenly observant with his patients and to wonder what might help **this** person. He began to trust that the same guidance he knew was part of his life could help him in discerning what was best for each patient. His intuition became more evident in his work and grew stronger in the following years.

Andrew investigated different models of health care, seeking to understand how chiropractors, naturopaths, psychologists, energy workers and anyone else he could find, viewed health and dis-ease. This broadened his view of health and the process of becoming unwell. Important lasting influences were his friendship with an energy worker in Horsham who provided most of the family's health care for a number of years and his connection with The Cairnmillar Institute in Melbourne. Cairnmillar provided psychological services and was run by the same Dr Francis Macnab who had impressed Andrew as a Uniting Church minister. Not only did Andrew learn new psychological approaches to human challenges like stress management but he developed close friendships with a number of the staff and eventually became a Board member of Cairnmillar for 2 years.

Through Andrew's involvement with WHI, he learned of The Emissaries, a spiritual group based in South Australia, where there was an intentional community at Riverdell. He and Lyell started attending courses there in the Art of Living and Spiritual Expression. Once again, friendships developed that would play an increasing part in both their lives over the coming decades.

The 1989 Spiritual Expression class had a marked impact on Andrew. He learned that true agreement is not a consensus or a mental concept. It could be felt in the body – a type of "yes, that's right" – an experience of another way of knowing what's true. He could not have predicted how important this would be in the months ahead.

These diverse influences all led to Andrew's growing confidence to try being different. He studied, and started implementing new methods of care via acupuncture, deeper counseling and nutritional medicine and almost inevitably, this led to increasing conflict with the medical colleagues within the group practice of which he was part.

Doctor Horwood began to realize that the deep "calling" he had been feeling all of these years was nothing less than a Divine invitation to uncover his true purpose in life. He had been led to accrue all of the tools he would need to fulfill his destiny. By virtue of being a country doctor, he had developed expertise in a wide variety of procedures that he would not have done in a city practice. This expanded his universe of patients and experience. Working with people's bodies was a way to connect with them. Working with their minds through his psychological skills, enabled them to discover they could move beyond the boundaries they had arbitrarily accepted for themselves. Working with their emotions enabled them to see how unresolved issues were impacting their ability to express themselves fully. Putting all of these elements together is what true healing is about –- guiding people to discover more about Life and experiencing greater fulfillment in the **now** through their own expression of Love in all of their relationships. He now saw that the starving Indian children he had seen in that documentary so many years ago represented people all over the world, in every walk of life, starving for love. Once again, it was a great theory and once again Life tested this out.

The Next Phase

The conflict within the group clinic was increasing. Help came in a very brief encounter with a resident of the Riverdell community. Andrew was rehashing his usual complaints about the limitations of life in that clinic. His listener told him that Life cannot align with you in the midst of complaint. He suggested that Andrew return to the clinic, own everything about the situation, **know** that there is nothing wrong and this is exactly where he should be. Be in that place as if there were nowhere else on earth he'd rather be. Take responsibility for it all and see what unfolds. Taking this advice to heart, Dr. Horwood returned to the clinic and opened himself to possibilities. He soon saw clearly where and how he could take a leadership role and offer his best to help resolve a conflict among the clinic staff. Like most fairy tales, this one had a twist – none of his partners agreed with his bright ideas!

Rather than seeing this as failure or the need to abandon his vision, Andrew saw this as a sign from the Divine that it was time to leave and create something new. Within three months, in February 1990, he had birthed Horsham Whole Health Clinic –- his own practice. Again, he saw how Life's design acted easily and for his own good when he surrendered to it. His partners amazingly waived the contract provision prohibiting any partner from opening a practice within 40km if they left the practice. They released him from this provision because they "knew" that his ideas were ridiculous and he would be a miserable failure in short order.

Another event ripped this new way of thinking out of the theoretical and put it right in his face demanding that he test the truth of it, thanks to Lyell.

In the year of his 40th birthday, Andrew was faced with the stark realization that the woman he loved was growing distant. She had become attracted to an itinerant dentist who wanted to whisk her away to the big city life of Melbourne. What he then saw as impending tragedy, he later recognized as a huge blessing in his life. It forced him to look at himself and what he was failing to offer to his wife. How could he ever be "savior to the world" if he couldn't even save his own marriage?

All this time he had dreamed of freeing people from their bonds of limitation so that they could rise up into the full expression of love that they were meant to be. Yet, where was his own experience of this love? He had little experience of it within his family growing up. When his mother came home from England upon the death of his father, he felt little compassion or love for her, even as he witnessed her grief. Somehow, he felt only anger towards her. Then the growing realizations during the 1980s had bean building a new capacity of heart inside him but this was not yet fully infusing his life. He realized he had been living a somewhat unconscious life with hopes that his intellectual pursuits and medical training would somehow move him up Maslow's pyramid. Now he saw the stark truth —- this inner compulsion to teach others to more fully express love in their lives was really a wake-up call to find that path for himself—- to embody Love. If he couldn't do that, then his dream was nothing but hollow grandiosity. But how to do it? Wishing it were true was not enough.

He was hugely thankful that Lyell was also interested in maintaining their relationship if he was willing to do the personal work necessary. He had no idea how hard that work would be. He would never have had the strength, patience, and courage to move through what turned out to be about four months that challenged his very Being if it weren't for the loving support that he received from friends at Riverdell. Andrew and Lyell could feel the creative tension every moment they were together and yet had no vision of what their new relationship would or should look like. There was no blueprint – no plan to follow – no examples in front of them. His friends just kept telling him to let go of any need to control the outcome, to release his fear, to know that there was nothing "wrong," that Life was doing something grand here, and to simply see what Life was sending to him.

Intuitively he felt the need for total surrender to Spirit in an admission that he could not resolve this issue with his vaunted intellect. He walked the streets of Horsham for hours at night doing nothing but reciting the Lord's Prayer and the 23rd Psalm over and over again. He released his desperation around his marriage entirely. Yes, he preferred that it would continue and grow stronger but he was willing to let it go it if that was the right thing to do. For the first time in his life, he prayed to God, "Thy Will be done" in total conviction and sincerity. The final revelation began with his first real experience of confession. He became consciously aware of something he had been deeply ashamed of for many years and he owned it totally. Then he went to Lyell and told her that he had been carrying this shame in his heart for years but had never shared it with her.

"That's it!" she exclaimed. She had felt for years that he had been withholding himself from her in some way without knowing what it was. It was that, and not the itinerant dentist, that was forcing her away from him. Now, in that moment of opening his heart and making it vulnerable, she had what she had longed for – the fullness of his love. Speaking of his shame broke the cursed spell of that shame. She embraced him like the prodigal son. What followed was several months of the most intimate, passionate love of their lives and another huge lesson learned in reality: the highest level of reward, true bliss, comes from living in honesty, openness, and sharing of the heart.

Prior to this dramatic happening in his life, he had hoped that he could lead people into this sense of freedom that he felt deep within himself was possible. After it, he **knew** his dream was possible because he had moved up Maslow's pyramid himself and not only tasted, but savored the freedom that he found. It was much more than he imagined. He felt like he was finally watching color TV after a lifetime of watching black and white and trying to visualize the colors. In this new paradigm of joy and creativity, he started writing poetry, harnessing his emotions, living in a place of inner peace, and **knowing** that Life indeed had a plan for him. Now he knew that this freedom that was vague to him before was freedom *from* all limitations and freedom *to* express life consistently in a joyful, peaceful, creative way.

Breaking New Ground

The death of his father – the threat to his marriage – the need to change his job. All of these helped him see clearly that seemingly disastrous events could serve as evolutionary steps with incredibly creative outcomes. This would only happen, however, if one could accept them and hold the creative tension, which often didn't feel very comfortable, allowing something new to work itself out. It was with this understanding of how creative processes work that Andrew designed his new medical practice.

He now knew that the traditional medical model was not leading people towards the freedom he knew was possible. Nor was the total answer to be found solely in psychology, chiropractic, or naturopathy, all of which he had investigated in his quest. He had started listening to his patients and found that ***they had their own answers inside of them.*** They just didn't know it. His job was to use all of the tools he had acquired to simply help them consciously discover the Truth of themselves.

Whereas most doctors spent 10 minutes with each patient, Andrew set up one hour appointments in his new clinic for new patients to allow for exploration of the patient's life rather than just their physical symptoms. Commonly, his patients would tell him, "I've never talked to anyone about these things and I certainly didn't expect to do so with you!" Some incredible things starting happening. As an example, one of his patients was a woman in her late forties suffering from fibromyalgia, TB, and anorexia along with severe depression. One of her three children had significant mental challenges and another had advanced Asperger Syndrome. There was great stress between her and her husband. In addition to medical advice, Dr. Horwood gave her a poem he had recently written that he felt would help her. She was deeply touched that he had sat with her for an hour, listening to her fears and had then given her this poem which spoke directly to her heart. She said that she felt welcomed home to a place where her heart could rest and she started to believe that there were other possibilities in her life than she had seen before. Over the ensuing fifteen years, all of her physical challenges healed and her relationship with each of her children and her husband changed dramatically.

A growing number of patients discovered that they could access greater possibilities in their lives than they had ever thought possible. Though he had seen similar results in a few patients during his nine years at Lister House Clinic, his revolutionary new approach was giving him a much more intimate look into his patients' lives and that was making a huge difference. Together, they went beyond physical symptoms to their deepest feeling issues, uncovering how the two were related.

Each patient was seen as a unique individual with specific needs. The goal in every case was to free them from limitations they had accepted so they might fully recognize and express the gifts they had to offer to the world. Some responded well to medical or complementary therapies, either alone or in combination. For others, counseling and emotional mastery training formed the major influence. Perhaps the greatest tool in Andrew's bag was simply spending time with each person and showing that he cared about them.

There was nothing better than watching people come alive and experience something glorious in their living. A woman in her sixties with bowel problems who had been in and out of hospitals for many years came free of her suffering when he showed her how it related to an inner tension that had dominated her life. Increasing her awareness of how to work with this, in addition to some terrific herbal remedies, resulted in long periods without hospitalization. Thus freed, this woman became a caregiver for an aged care center and experienced a richness in her life she hadn't felt in 15 years.

Andrew continued in his quest to increase his capacity to fulfill his highest vision for wholeness. He would say: "what's possible for this person is not only limited by their consciousness but mine as well." He took responsibility for expanding *his* consciousness through study and experience so that he had more to offer.

He bathed in several pivotal influences during the next evolutionary steps in the 1990s. Andrew had discovered the great value of emotional mastery in 1994 when he began studying with Nicholas de Castella on emotional intelligence. He immediately saw the tremendous value of emotional mastery and the part it played in holistic health. He continued his relationship with de Castella for sixteen years, honing his understanding of how to help people with it. This was a practice with which patients could continue working and go to great depth, discovering a source of energy, peace, and love within them that had been lost to them. A nurse came to Andrew with a long history of back problems. Primarily through emotional mastery work and personal mentoring, she discovered a whole new experience of life and is now one of the leading providers of Tantra counseling herself, in position to help many others.

Andrew met an inspiring Professor of General Practice, the late Ian McWhinney, who was visiting the Family Medicine Program from Canada. Prof McWhinney authored "The Patient Centred Clinical Method", a wonderful description of holistic medicine in a traditional general practice setting. A deep friendship began in which Andrew and Ian shared a rich correspondence, with Ian encouraging Andrew to pursue his dreams of what medical practice could be.

Horsham was also blessed with others who shared Andrew's holistic views. A key colleague was Des Lardner, pharmacist, naturopath and herbalist with whom Andrew could not only share mutual support, but also actively collaborate on patient care. Their partnership brought a great blessing to many patients and enabled Andrew to use a range of specialized therapies not widely available.

Throughout the 1990s, Andrew and Lyell's involvement with The Emissaries at Riverdell deepened. This group had a generous vision of spirituality, about each of us becoming the full Being we were born to be, living that and in so doing, bring our gift to the world. The Horwoods visited Riverdell twice yearly and held Emissary meetings regularly, hosting local and overseas guests and including the energy practice called attunement. This gradually built a stronger and stronger practical spiritual foundation in their lives.

Creating the Environment

For his new healing model to work, there needed to be an energy field of personal support, growth, and creativity present from the time the patient walked in the door for the first time. To provide this, Andrew gathered a group of people around him in a co-creative environment, each one of the six employees accepting that they were part of the healing experience. Andrew had created the clinic within his home. The reception area was a lounge room providing a warm, comfortable invitation to an intimate experience. The receptionist was the "first part of their treatment" as opposed to someone greeting them, making appointments, and taking payments. Through this first interaction, the patient developed a trusted friend and was already at ease when they met with the practice nurse or Dr. Horwood. The combination of doctor and nurse working closely together created a container for greater care of each patient. Office planning sessions were held every fortnight and they took time to consider, not only practice issues, but what was happening in each of their lives. Nurturing themselves provided the comfortable, growing environment they sought for the patients.

Add to this loving environment a full range of therapies including vitamins and minerals, intravenous Vitamin C therapy, acupuncture, bio-energetic medicine, homeopathy, counseling, breathing instruction, and more traditional medical treatments plus collaboration with specialists in psychiatry, hypnotherapy and energy balancing, who came into the clinic to see patients. Excitement reigned as they constantly explored new areas of healing.

Financial return was secondary to establishing this type of care at an affordable price, yet Dr. Horwood never felt like there was any personal sacrifice. He knew it was the right way to run a practice and experienced much greater personal fulfillment than he ever had when making more money at the former Clinic. Here indeed was bliss.

End of an Era

Seems like the end of a perfect fairy tale, right? But one thing that Andrew had learned is that Life never stagnates. After about ten years, there was the feel of change in the air. Staff at the practice sensed it, yet nobody could define it. They discussed it at the office planning sessions and thought that maybe it was time to grow to the next level. After all, they had an investor willing to lend $500,000 to build a new, larger clinic so it would have been easy to move in that direction. By now, the whole team was aware of the nature of creative cycles and the need to let pressure build before the right solution would present itself. So they continued the practice as is, but with everyone staying alert for signs of the next step. Before too long, Andrew and Lyell began to feel like it might be time to close the practice, take a break, and see where Life would lead them next. They didn't act on that sensing at that time but it was a portent of things to come.

In 2006, the sign came to them in the form of a gall bladder attack (Life doesn't always give us signs in pleasant ways!). Following the surgery, Andrew had a "peak experience." Even though he was aware of pain, he also felt he was being held in a cocoon of the most exquisite golden love. At first, he thought it might be a product of the morphine drip but then he saw that it had never been turned on!! He knew it was an act of Grace, revealing to him the experience of the loving support available for him in whatever he would do. He and Lyell now knew that they were to close the practice. Within weeks, he saw an ad for a new clinic planning to open in Horsham in 2-3 months. Here was the perfect exit strategy. Though he had concern for his employees and the level of care that his patients would receive, he knew deep in his Being that this was the right thing to do.

What to do about his beloved employees? Andrew felt sure that, if this was the right direction, then all would work out perfectly. The day after his meeting with the new clinic owners, his practice nurse asked for a meeting. Though he hadn't announced the plan to close the clinic, Andrew brought champagne to the meeting, knowing that it was a time to celebrate the next phase for all involved. Lo and behold – the nurse and her partner had just decided to move to another state so she was agonizing over leaving the practice and how to tell Andrew and Lyell ! She was gobsmacked and delighted when Andrew told her his news. All of the staff easily found other work and the patients had a smooth transition to new medical care. Within six weeks of meeting with the new clinic owners, everything was complete. Those involved described it as an easy, blissful experience like riding the crest of a wave. Rather than bemoaning the closing of a clinic, they threw a party inviting all staff and patients and celebrated the close of a wonderful 16 year cycle called the Horsham Whole Health Clinic.

The Current Chapter

Having gloriously brought that cycle to a close, the question now was, "What's next?" It wasn't clear to Andrew and Lyell at all. In June 2006, in desperation they asked each other "Where will you go to live if I die?" When each had the same answer, Riverdell, the path was laid for their next step: "Why not move there now, while we're both still alive?" It would be perfect. They could enjoy a semi-retirement, working a bit in the beautiful surround of Riverdell and spending the rest of their time in Victoria catching up with family and friends. Andrew had been feeling for some time the need for introspection which he knew would lead to his next phase of spiritual growth and yet he hadn't been able to take that time while running his practice. Being far from home and family, Riverdell would be the perfect place. He was sure it would be a place of supportive friendship, comfort, and peace. Once again, a nice theory that Life would test out.

The small community at Riverdell welcomed Andrew and Lyell and offered employment. There were changes afoot at Riverdell within the community which, while unfolding as changes do, created an environment of some angst and insecurity for Andrew – anything but the womb experience he had expected. In addition to the external changes, Andrew knew this time of introspection would go deep but he didn't anticipate just how deep! His mother had given him the nickname "Joe" when he was a baby. She said that when he was upset, she'd say "hold on Joe", and this would immediately delight him. So that name stuck – throughout his life. Andrew enjoyed it as it gave him a way of being different from the birth name he'd been given. There was a rebellious element in his use of that name. Joe was another personality to Andrew –- a bit exhibitionist, wild, unconventional and with a sense of immaturity. This personality had served him well and yet he felt it might be time for a change. He sensed that there was a deeper, more mature personality waiting to emerge if it had a chance.

A wise woman had said to him years before "at some stage, you'll go back to your birth name." He nodded politely but didn't take it seriously. Now, in this period of introspection, this name change, which also signified an identity change, surfaced again. Within a few months of moving to Riverdell, Andrew found himself in the middle of a workshop asked to make a declaration about who he was. In that moment, he realized this was the time to re-own his birth name. He stepped into the centre of the circle and declared, "my name is Andrew Horwood," and asked all present to call him that. He didn't anticipate what this identity change would require of him, nor of the important people in his life who had no warning that this name change was going to happen!

This convergence of both inner and outer changes really challenged Andrew's resources. He became very disoriented and entered the most anxious and depressed six-month period of his entire life. Simple conversations baffled him. He started having palpitations and not sleeping at night. He made the mistake of self-diagnosing and put himself on an alkalizing diet with bicarbonate of soda. Figuring if a little was good, a lot would be better, he overdosed and almost poisoned himself by lowering his potassium to a dangerously low level. Every attempt at a medical solution made it worse. About to start himself on anti-depressants, he had a life-changing conversation on the phone with a spiritual mentor. This trusted advisor reminded him that he was merely in a "water cycle" – a time of transition when things were unclear as factors were still forming that would lead to his next creative stage if he remained still and open to it. Well DUH!! Why hadn't he seen it? This was the same process he had gone through regarding his relationship with Lyell and again with the transformation of his business. His clarity had been derailed by the disillusionment of how he thought life would be at Riverdell. That had been caused by his own expectations which closed him off from co-creating with what Life had in mind. Ah ha –- he could remember now –- let go and let God.

The disintegrating cycle having to do with letting go continued for 2 years and was concurrent with new learning and an integrative, creative process that led to a deepening trust in the way Life works. He learned how to hold a container, for himself as well as others, to let the design from the invisible (Heaven) be planted and nurtured in the visible (Earth) rather than second-guessing what he thought should be happening. He learned how to move through a time when things seemed to be falling apart without being distracted by the intensity, being willing to continue to say YES to that which was revealing itself to him. He learned that he could accept even the deep depression he had fallen into if that was part of a creative outworking without judging it as bad or wrong. Life was preparing him for what was next.

When they had arrived at Riverdell in 2007, there were two leaders of the community. One vacated his post shortly after Lyell and Andrew arrived. The other stepped down in 2011. The community was considering whether they should disband. All of the learning that Andrew had gone through in that four years, along with Lyell, brought them to the point where they knew in their hearts that it was their place to take the leadership role at Riverdell and keep it alive.

That is why the white-haired man with the penetrating eyes and incandescent smile will be greeting you should you visit Riverdell today. He has found a higher level to Maslow's pyramid where he can help people find the freedom he only felt in his bones as a twelve-year-old. The people in the Riverdell community are literally loving themselves into greatness and inviting anyone who visits to have a lasting experience of larger and larger possibilities in their lives through knowing the reality of Love filling them from the inside. His fulfillment is in sharing the very art of living fully with those who live, work and visit Riverdell and watching their lives blossom. Whereas the medical model taught him how to see and work with what was wrong with people — dis-ease — he was now seeing through the eyes of Love what was right with people as the starting point. This was the next experience of bliss Life had in store.

Maslow said "What a man can be, he must be. This need we call self-actualization." This is what it means to fulfill one's potential. When one does this, you end up with a 1000 watt smile and eyes that warm the soul.

PostScript

A story such as this is not the end of the movie. Life continues to call each of us to new adventures, and so it is with Andrew. With both children now married and living in Melbourne, 450 miles away, Andrew knew that grandchildren were on the way and, with that, the call to return to Melbourne. He wants to be an actively involved grandparent, as does Lyell. In April 2015, their grandson, James, was born and planning for that move ramped up. They purchased a small apartment close to their daughter for easy visiting.

Knowing that a succession plan was needed to secure Riverdell's future, the Emissary Board created a strategic plan which acknowledged that there would be an upcoming need for new leadership.

The details of how this transition process for both Riverdell and the Horwoods will work out are not clear. Once again, the key elements are following an inner calling of Spirit and trusting that the design for this transition will reveal itself over time. With everything that Andrew has learned about life, he's embracing this change with trust, confidence and inner peace, knowing that yet more bliss awaits.

INTRODUCTION TO "THE UGLY SWEATER"

Conventional wisdom would have you plan the path to your dream job. When I worked for General Electric in the 70's, a Human Resources person would come out once/year and sit down with each of us to review our one year, five year, and ten year plans for our career. I never did any of those plans, and I went on to have an awesome, award-winning, lucrative, and very fulfilling career. Twists and turns in it were often determined by factors that I had no way to ever plan.

You never really know what might launch you in the right direction. If you read my first book, *Journaling the Journey: 25 Spiritual Insights to Light The Way*, then you know I was put on my career path by a telephone pole. Sometimes the path to our dream job has a really strange starting line – like an ugly sweater. Meet Gary Winkler........

THE UGLY SWEATER

as told by Gary Winkler

I grew up a Yankees fan…Dad was a Mets fan (desperate convert when the Brooklyn Dodgers skipped town after the '57 season). I cheered on the Nets, while he rooted for the Knicks. I championed the Jets, while he was wearing Giants' colors. Neither one of us cared about hockey, so that wasn't an issue. This refusal to follow in my father's cleats was the only evidence that my older sister, Amy, and I shared the same genetic code. She was the independent one and pretty much set her own path in every part of her life. She never intentionally tried to give our parents heartburn. She merely had her own way of thinking and wasn't hindered by a deep desire to please other people, including parental people. I was the very conservative, goodie-goodie, stayed-out-of-trouble kid who never needed a curfew and was a stranger to those "my house/my rules" conversations that are carefully outlined in the "Parenting Teenagers for Dummies" handbook. So my version of rebelling revealed itself in the relatively safe dominion of sports teams. Truth be told, Dad actually supported my teams and watched all their games with me regardless.

Of course, like every sports-junkie kid, I not only wanted to watch sports; I dreamed of growing up and, in my case, playing in the NBA. I could almost see myself as I windmilled a slam dunk at the buzzer to crush the Lakers and take home the Larry O'Brien Championship trophy for the Nets. In baseball, I was never much of a hitter, but I had a great arm at a very young age so I played third base for a while (one of the few kids that could actually get the ball to first on a fly). Then I had a magical year at 8 years old as the phenom pitcher that was striking everyone out. I played basketball with the big kids on the street and held my own. My dreams were getting more vivid and in technicolor. Things went downhill from there, however, as everybody else kept growing far more in height and talent than I did. Alas, my sports abilities peaked at nine years old. Facing physical reality, my passion morphed from BEING an athlete to talking about athletes.

Introduction to Radio

My new obsession with becoming a sports announcer kindled a desire to set up my own booth in my parent's basement so I could begin practicing. A basic set of DJ equipment sold for $1500. Of course, I didn't **have** $1500 or anything close to it. Asking my parents for $1500 so I could play pretend sports announcer was not in the cards for me. Enter WPLJ. This was a popular Top 40 radio station in the area that I used to listen to all the time — not just for the music, mind you, but to enter the contests. Having no other life and being determined, I actually won 7 times! One time it was tickets to a Salt-N-Pepa and Nu Shooz concert. Of course, they were playing in a club that served alcohol and I was under 21, so I couldn't even go! The people at the station sent me their cassette tapes instead. There were other prizes like that, and once I even won $95 in cash! Nice, but hardly enough to launch my career. Then I hit the jackpot - $1000!! That got me in the ballpark. I was able to scrape together the rest, and WOTA was born. That was the name I gave to my imaginary radio station. The OTA stood for On The Air. Of course, I **wasn't** on the air but that didn't stop me from recording made-up shows and broadcasting non-existent games.

Turns out that this wasn't entirely useless. Word got out that I had equipment and some talent and someone asked me to DJ a party. What fun! AND I got paid for it. I called my DJ company "On The Air DJs."

The $25/hour I got paid didn't go far. After paying a buddy $30 for helping and covering about $50 in costs, I think I made all of about $20 from my first gig. Now, however, I had a career path, and I was only a high school sophomore. I felt like I was on my way to the broadcasting career of my dreams.

The sports-announcer passion then morphed into simply being an announcer of some sort. Becoming a DJ was filling the bill and lining my pockets. The ultimate dream hadn't changed. I could see that I was on a path that might help me get there. Now it was all about being the best DJ I could be. One professional DJ on WPLJ that I idolized was Bobby Valentine. It didn't hurt that he had the same name as a baseball player/manager, but I found out later that it wasn't actually his given name. Strike one for Bobby, but I still loved him as a DJ. Lo and behold, it turned out that he lived in Manalapan - my town! Even more surprising - he agreed to let me interview him. I was on cloud 9! The interview went really well. I wrote up a story for my school paper *which they didn't print*!! I was shocked. Though I was fuming at the time, it actually turned out well. The local Manalapan paper heard about it and did a story about my obsession with being a DJ, the opportunity to interview Bobby V. and the twist of my school paper "dissing" the story. I now had the first press coverage of my career.

The St. John's Connection

By now, you are probably wondering what all of this has to do with an ugly sweater. Well, we're getting there. First, I have to weave in another aspect of the story - my passion for St. John's basketball. How did a Jewish kid become such a big fan of St John's, a Catholic school? Glad you asked. Early on, I was drawn to college basketball because they were passionate about the game rather than the money. St. John's was the local team and stars like Mark Jackson, Walter Berry, and Chris Mullin made for some very exciting basketball. 1985 saw them go to the Final Four and that's when I got totally hooked on them and their coach. The rival back then was Georgetown whose coach was John Thompson, a man who always wore a suit and tie. He was a tall, serious, no-nonsense coach.

St. John's was led by Lou Carnesecca, a passionate, animated guy with an outrageous sense of humor and this wild sweater collection. Though unconventional as a college coach, "Looie" led St. John's to the post-season every year he coached them. I became obsessed with Carnesecca and St. John's basketball.

Now we can talk about "the sweater." It was originally knitted by my grandmother for my sister, Amy. Having wonderful flair but not much sense of modern style, Grandma Ruth used bright, fluorescent-colored yarn that blended many colors, one after another— hot pink, safety orange, highlighter yellow, electric lime, turquoise, bright purple, then back to hot pink — giving the sweater a mottled look. It was open in the front, had 3/4 length sleeves, strings with tassels to tie up near the neck and crocheted edging. Grandma lived in Florida as did our cousin Dana who was entrusted to deliver the sweater to Amy when she traveled up to NJ with her parents for my Bar Mitzvah. As Dana handed it to Amy saying, "Grandma made this for YOU," the "I'm-so-glad-it's-not-for-me" tone so well crafted by little girls was unmistakable. Amy dutifully called Grandma Ruth to thank her for the wonderful gift and then threw the sweater on to a shelf in her closet, never to emerge. She hated it from the moment she saw it and had no intention of even trying it on.

I don't remember exactly when I got the inspiration to wear it as the "good luck" sweater while watching St John's games with high school friends in my basement, but it became a big hit and a tradition. It followed me to Rutgers where it was heartily embraced by new college friends and made for some occasional dorm laughs. It became the thing in the dorm for other guys to wear it after coming back from sports bars (we all had fake ID's of course) where we had watched the game. The sleeves barely reached our elbows. The string ties looked absolutely ridiculous on a guy. I'm not sure they looked much better on a girl! As a freshman at Rutgers, I still had a Madison Square Garden season ticket plan (5-7 games) for seats way up in the nose bleed section for St. John's hoops. Friends always tried to get me to wear the sweater to the games but I never had the nerve to wear it outside of the dorm.

Lou Carnesecca was in his final year of coaching for SJU in March of '92, and Madison Square Garden ran a promotion honoring his tradition of wearing sweaters vs. suits. The fan who attended the game wearing the "most outrageous sweater" would win a trip to Florida. My buddies would not let me pass up this opportunity. I couldn't see myself riding the NJ Transit train wearing this testament to poor taste, so I brought the sweater in a bag.

That day, those of us interested in being part of the contest came into the Paramount lobby and walked a closed door runway in front of a panel of three judges. Five of us were selected out of maybe two hundred people to go on court at halftime to "strut our stuff." I couldn't believe I made the cut! Noticing that a really attractive woman was in our final five, I figured the winner was a foregone conclusion. As we went out, each of us walked around the floor trying to get the crowd on our side as the selection was to be done by crowd response. After a short time, a judge would stand behind each of us, one at a time, and ask the crowd to applaud, indicating their vote. I think I got more laughter than applause with people wondering, "What is that??" Nobody could believe anyone would wear that sweater. Though it might have been more raucous laughter than clapping, it was still obvious that I got the biggest response, far more even than the lovely lady I thought would be the winner. Each of the five of us took home an autographed Looie shirt, and I won a trip to Ft. Lauderdale for spring break. So it really **was** a lucky sweater, at least for me. Not so much for St. John's who lost that day.

The sweater went on to get air time. Billy Packer showed the sweater on the TV broadcast and said, "This was the winner of the Most Outrageous Sweater Contest. Personally, I wouldn't wash a car with this," and threw it on the floor. Then he went back to announcing the game. On the Monday following the game, I did a radio interview by telephone with John Gambling (WOR "Rambling with Gambling") where, sadly, the host kept referring to it as the "ugliest sweater contest." Thus was born the Legend of the Ugly Sweater.

The Path to My Dream Job

Having already made arrangements to go to Canada with friends (what was I thinking? Who goes to Canada for spring break?), I was unable to cash in my prize that year. Having to reschedule the trip to the following year required me to coordinate with the promotions folks at Madison Square Garden. I spoke to one woman about four times and developed a nice relationship with her, learning about internships in the process. We'll come back to that.

My degree from Rutgers is in Environmental Business and Economics. Dad had suggested that as a solid career path to follow; but for me, it was designed to give me a fallback position. I never had any real interest in any of it. Though I had made good grades in high school, nobody would have identified me as a great student in college. My passion was all about sports and being on the air. I was much more focused on sports announcing than college courses. My formal studies had zero impact on my eventual career. This is not to say that college wasn't a valuable experience. Rutgers is where I cut my teeth as a serious DJ and college sports announcer. I learned so much about behind-the-scenes production and radio. I developed proficiency in timing, organization and working with people.

Being a sports announcer for the Rutgers student radio station created some interesting moments for me. In addition to my fervor for St. John's basketball, I was also a Penn State football fan. Apparently I didn't hide my allegiances all that well while announcing a Penn State-Rutgers game. Screaming any time Penn State graced the end zone led some Rutgers students to wonder if they were listening to the Penn State announcers! OK — so maybe it was only the three people actually listening to our station that might have felt that way.

It certainly didn't pay but it was the most fun I had had in this broadcast hobby to date. My obsession with sports fully transformed into broadcasting during this time. I had given up my desire to head to nice, warm Florida for college, where girls playing volleyball in bikinis would not have helped my odds for graduation. I chose, instead, to continue developing my DJ career in NJ. It paid off with a brief professional stint working on-air for a local station in central Jersey. I got some amazing experience reporting live ("stringing") from high school football games, anchored sports updates from the studio and even got to interview a couple of Jets (at a pre-season game). The Sports Director put a lot of faith in me and gave me a shot while I was actually still in college. For sure, he was an important person in my career. I learned a lot from him and got some amazing experience in the "biz."

Now back to that intern thing. The promotions woman I had worked with connected me with Madison Square Garden's HR folks who told me all about their internship program. That got me an interview with a vice-president of the Knicks. My nervousness dissolved as we had such an easy, casual, personal interview: "What are your interests? Who are your favorite announcers? . . ." Just like that, I was a NY Knicks intern! OK, so I wasn't going to be the play-by-play guy for the team, but I saw this as a good opportunity to be in some aspect of sports. Who knew where it might lead me. It was 1994. The Knicks went to the finals that year, losing to Olajuwon and the Rockets in 7 games after being ahead 3 games to 2 going to Houston. Meanwhile, in hockey, the Rangers won the Stanley Cup. Not many college juniors experienced the excitement of being around that amazing NYC atmosphere. Never mind that I didn't really care about or understand much about hockey. This was a dream come true. It just didn't get any better than this!

Once again, I wasn't really making any money; but I was gaining a ton of experience. As my senior year rolled around, the Knicks made me an offer to come on board as a sports trainee (paid intern). My heart said YES, but my brain decided I should finish school. I kept my hand in it by working on about a dozen home games in the marketing department. Part of my invaluable services included stuffing envelopes for a mailing, but I would have done anything to stay in the mix. I just *hoped* they would make me an offer when I graduated.

May came and I did, in fact, graduate. A week went by. Then two. Then a month. I was preparing to send out my demo tapes to radio stations in hot spots like Kalispell, Montana and Alton, Iowa. In my heart, however, I knew that I was destined to join the New York Knicks. By the end of the summer, like most college kids, I was out of school and still jobless.

Surrendering my position of sitting by the phone waiting for the Knicks to call, I went on vacation with my girlfriend's family. We drove down to Myrtle Beach to enjoy the sun and sand. She and I were out fairly late one night. When we got back, her parents were waiting up for us. Not usually a good sign; but in this case, her Mom just said, "Call your Mom. Doesn't matter how late it is." Worried about what it could be, I was at first relieved and then totally excited when she told me that the Knicks had called and wanted me to interview with the president the next day! I could barely sleep that night. My girlfriend's dad drove me to the airport in Myrtle Beach the next morning. My dad and grandmother picked me up at Laguardia Airport in NY with some proper clothes and rushed me to Manhattan. I did a Superman change in the back seat of the car and made it to the interview with little time to spare.

Fulfilling The Dream

That frantic rush to make an interview turned into fourteen years with the Knicks. I worked 5-6 days and 60+ hrs/week and loved every minute. When we added the WNBA New York Liberty in 1997, I would be working a game in the summer while my better half was calling me from the beach. I, however, loved the work and living the dream of being around professional sports. No way would I have traded that for the beach.

Without really noticing how it happened, by 2005, I found myself as the Knick's Vice President of Event Presentation in charge of music, lighting, dance team, contests — virtually everything other than the game. I felt like I was a guy with no talent except the ability to coordinate incredibly-talented players, dancers, video editors, lighting guys, sound guys, etc. It felt to me like conducting an orchestra. I loved organizing the preparations for an event. From needing to know exactly when to stop the music as TV came back from commercials, switch cameras, get the half-time show on and off the court, and dozens of other details, I developed an obsession with timing. To this day, I time everything that I do — how long it takes to get to work, how long it takes for food deliveries, how long I walk the dog. Early on, I still had aspirations of announcing, but ultimately fell in love with behind the scenes production; and now I worked alongside the play-by-play guys I had once wanted to be.

Not many people "fall into" a career that they love. I, therefore, give great thanks to Grandma Ruth and her "ugly sweater," the entry to my dream career.

__Postscript__

Gary left the Knicks in 2008, and is now with the Times Square Alliance. This is an organization that works to improve and promote Times Square by cultivating the creativity, energy and edge that have made the area an icon of entertainment, culture and urban life for over a century. In addition to providing core neighborhood services with its Public Safety Officers and Sanitation Associates, the Alliance promotes local businesses, encourages economic development and public improvements, and co-coordinates the major events in Times Square. This includes the annual New Year's Eve celebration and the world-famous dropping of the ball. Gary found that his true passion was the organizational skills he had developed within the framework of the sports world. Those skills also came into play in his new position. So, even though he has left his beloved sports arena, he *still* loves what he is doing.

He is also still timing everything!

INTRODUCTION TO "LED BY THE HAND OF GOD"

There are many ways to discover your passion in life.

Some people seem to come out of the womb knowing their destiny. Others, like me, find it through a "chance" encounter (see my first book for the telephone pole story). Maybe your father, his father, and his father, along with two sisters, an uncle and two cousins were all mechanics, and you were raised in a garage with a wrench in your hand intuitively knowing that the problem with this '76 Ford Torino is a loose ignition coil (like the Marisa Tomei character in *My Cousin Vinny* which, by the way, is a must-see movie). Perhaps watching an old re-run of *Perry Mason* with your grandfather struck a chord deep inside of you which initiated your quest to become a lawyer.

Then there are times when necessity is the mother of invention. Actually, in this case, that would be the mother of discovery; but I don't know of an old saying that covers that. When one is desperate for a job, any job will do. Once in a while, that act of desperation leads you to your passion. Meet Leon Keenan............

LED BY THE HAND OF GOD

While visiting my friend Louise in South Africa, I agreed to go with her to have her hair done. On the forty-five minute ride that followed, we must have passed 100 or more perfectly competent hairdressers. I knew some were of the Super Cuts inexpensive variety while others were chi-chi, boutique-style salons beyond the pocketbook of most women. Many others filled the gap in between. Were we just taking this long ride so we could enjoy the Johannesburg scenery? When the question was put to Louise, she told me that she simply adored Leon as a person. In addition, nobody else styled her hair quite as well as he had been doing for many years, ever since she lived much closer to his shop. Most often, she did go to someone in her neighborhood but there were those times when she felt she just had to give herself and her hair a treat. That meant packing a lunch, gassing up the car, and trekking to Leon.

Being bald, I didn't get the pleasure of sampling Leon's skills personally, but I did see immediately why she was drawn to this charming, upbeat, vivacious man. As she sat with her hair in foil, I had the opportunity to chat a bit with Leon and asked him how he had gotten started as a hairdresser. Sometimes simple questions lead to wonderful stories.

The Beginning

Born in Johannesburg to an Irish father (Edward John Keenan) and a South African mother (Johanna Welhelmina Vorster), who was the granddaughter of the famous South African General De la Ray, Leon moved with his family to Northern Rhodesia (now Zambia) while still a baby. There, his father found work first as a cinema operator and later in the copper mines where the work was more dangerous but paid better.

Life took a dramatic turn for Leon when he was only ten years old. A friend had undergone open heart surgery. Leon was given permission to go on holiday with that boy's family in Durban, South Africa during his recovery. For this reason, Leon was not with his family when the tires of their car hit the edge of a strip road and blew out. This caused the car to roll three times, killing his mother, seven year-old brother Desmond Gene, and five year-old sister Margaret Ann and paralyzing his dad from the waist down.

Having had no prior notice of the incident, he was overcome with traumatic grief when, upon his departure from the Durban train, he learned of the accident. He was horrified to find out that his family had lain in the road for eight hours outside of a small remote village between their home and Victoria Falls where the family had been on holiday. His little sister had actually been buried there by the villagers. Her body had to be exhumed so she could be transported back home to be buried with her mother and brother. This burial happened before Leon returned, so he was not even able to say goodbye at the funeral.

Edward Keenan recovered from his paralysis after three months and was physically able to return to work, but life would never return to normal. The grief and guilt that he struggled with, though the accident was not his fault, never left him; and he was emotionally unable to raise his one remaining child. Leon would go to the mines every day with his dad and attend a school there, trying to establish some sense of normalcy. He had no place to go for lunch so he was the only child to eat with the miners. He went to swimming classes in the afternoons to try to distract himself from the horror that had befallen his family. His dad would come home at five but had little to offer in the way of comfort. Edward remarried, but it was a troubled household and Leon was sent to an orphanage when he was twelve years old.

Finding Family

As Leon was to find throughout his life, God works in very mysterious ways. Prior to being sent to the orphanage, he went with his step-mother to spend some time with her brother in Johannesburg. He knew that his birth mother had six sisters and six brothers there but, having no contact information, there didn't seem to be any hope of finding them. One of his aunts was a very religious Christian and had been praying to reconnect with Leon. Walking outside one day, Leon saw an old two-tone Chevy parked across the street. It had big tail fins and a Zulu doll hanging from the mirror. The car looked so familiar to him that he went over and asked the children in the car who they were. Amazingly, it belonged to his aunt who was visiting her mother-in-law whose home was on that block. Leon had only seen that car when he was about two years old. Though he would not have recognized his aunt if he had seen her, the misty memory of that old Chevy reunited them. Still, it was to be several more years before they spent much time together. Shortly after that day, Leon returned to Rhodesia where, after a brief time, he was sent to the orphanage.

Freedom

Northern Rhodesia became Zambia when they gained their independence from Great Britain in 1964. One might say that Leon gained his independence that same year as he ran away from the orphanage where he had lived for two years.

Having nowhere else to go, he hitchhiked and walked the 1200 miles (1900 km) from Luanshya, Zambia to Johannesburg (known as Joburg to the locals) where he had hopes of living with the aunt he had miraculously found. The trip was not without its perils. One man who gave him a ride offered to put him up for the night. Having no money and being innocent to the ways of the world, Leon was open to that. There was, however, another youth who had also hitched a ride. He was more street-savvy and could sense the less-than-honorable intentions of the driver. He told Leon he would pay for a hotel room so Leon spent the night in safety. The rest of the trip was without incident.

Knowing that the truth would get him turned away at the border, he told South African Immigration officials that he was an orphaned refugee from the Belgian Congo and that all of his papers had been lost during the coups. Since 100,000 people had been killed in this uprising resulting in hordes of refugees, his story was believable; and he was accepted into the country. Lying about his age, he managed to land a job packing shoes for Mosenthals, a large clothing wholesaler who exported their product all over the world. He was not successful in connecting with any of his aunts and uncles then, but he managed to get a boarding house room in Judith's Paarl. Hardly palatial, this facility had a common kitchen and bath; and there were as many as six people sleeping in each of the seven rooms. The attraction of this boarding house was that the rent was only three pounds per month. The landlady was nice to him. Finding this place was another example to Leon that "someone up there" was looking after him.

After two years, Mosenthals merged with a larger company, Jagers. They liked Leon and wanted to keep him on; but in the process, his real age was uncovered. An older couple that worked there warned him that people from the Welfare Department were coming to get him. They just happened to mention that his check was ready, and he might want to grab it and be gone before the government agents came calling. Heeding their advice, he collected his money, quickly packed up and left South Africa, hitchhiking and walking back to Zambia. Unable to locate his father, who had moved, Leon went to the town of Bancroft (now known as Chililabambwe). Friends, who now lived there, had invited him to move in with them. This was on the Congo border in Zambia's copperbelt district, and he thought he could easily get a job in the mines there. Even though he had now turned sixteen and was of legal working age, he had no schooling and every door was closed to him. After having no luck with the mines, he tried the railways, clothing stores, and everything else he could think of without success.

One day while walking the streets, he saw a sign in a hairdresser's shop, "Apprentice Wanted". He eagerly accepted the job though he knew nothing about the business. There was no hint in his mind of the huge impact this decision would have on the rest of his life as he started out sweeping the floors and doing shampoos. Another guardian angel entered his life in the form of Polly Tyler, the shop owner. She took an instant liking to Leon and, after a while, allowed him to work on clients even though he was not licensed to do so. She saw that he had a knack for it and the clients enjoyed him as much as he enjoyed interacting with them. After a year and a half, she decided he should pursue his certification. Since there were no colleges for hairdressing in Zambia, Polly arranged for Leon to attend college in Johannesburg. She even got him a job with someone she knew there so he could work three days per week to support himself while going to school.

A Lifelong Passion

Working at the salon in Joburg and attending the four year hairdressing college deepened Leon's love for this work. What had started out as the only way he could find to earn a paycheck had turned into a full-blown passion. He loved everything about the business with his favorite part being the interaction with his clients. He couldn't imagine wanting to make his living any other way. By the end of the second year, the owner was allowing him to take clients on his own. As with Polly, the owner, a Hungarian woman named Irene, saw his love for the business and his increasing skills and disregarded the fact that he was not yet licensed.

Upon graduation, Leon became a full-time hairdresser at Salon Irene and hit the ground running since he already had an established client base. After two years working closely with Irene, tragedy struck around Leon again. Her life outside the shop had serious challenges, and Irene's ultimate solution was suicide. Though her death shook him, Leon had learned at an early age that death is a part of life to be accepted. He moved on to another salon, Raymond and Harth. There he flourished, buying the shop as a young man after working there for five years. He renamed the business Salon Renee after his partner, an Austrian woman. The two of them thrived in business for 28 years. Renee's husband, Gerti, was killed in an auto accident just as they were preparing to go on holiday. Renee had no interest in working anymore, and Leon didn't want to run the shop alone so they sold the salon. Since then, he has worked in three salons with many of his loyal clients following him.

Talk with his clients and the words that keep coming up to describe Leon are caring, loving, and special. It is not unusual for two or even three generations of a family to be going to Leon to get their hair done. Bev and Pam started getting their hair done by Leon when they were about 7-9 years old which made them feel like the "bees' knees." Their Mom had a job that required her to look professional at all times. While Mom was having her hair done three times per week, the girls would be "helping" by passing rollers, combs, and whatever else was needed to their friend, Leon. He loved having them there, and they loved being there. Eighteen years later, he was doing Bev's hair for her wedding. The incredible job he did still made her feel like the bees' knees. He teased it up so high, in the style of the day, that she thought it would never come down. Everybody talked about how perfect her hair was. Not surprising since Leon was a perfectionist. He couldn't stand it if a single hair was out of place. He may not have been in the high-priced part of town or charged those prices; but when you left his salon, you looked like you were coming out of a salon in Sandton (affluent area of Joburg).

Somehow, between their moves and his, the girls lost touch with Leon and began to go to the fancy salons that their friends recommended. It was just never the same. After some years of paying much higher prices and not getting anywhere near the caring treatment they were used to with Leon, they started wondering if he was still in business. Being very determined and resourceful, they tracked him down. "Returning to Leon was like coming back to family," Bev told me. "The higher-priced salons didn't really care about me. They just did whatever they thought would be good for me but they didn't really know me. Leon may be old-school and not have a fancy salon or be in a wealthy neighborhood; but when I go there, I get hugs and kisses when I come in and when I leave. I'm always feeling so much better than when I went in."

Pam told me, "Leon is a loving, caring, beautiful man who doesn't just do hair. He makes you feel special, and you know he considers you family. It's so important to him that you leave not only satisfied but very happy with the way you look." She loves the way that he makes suggestions and then they have back and forth discussions. If she is hesitant to try a new color he suggests, he tells her, "Let's just try it for fun. If you don't like it, I'll change it back for you." If she asks for something, he's not afraid to tell her if he thinks it wouldn't be right for her. He has a knack for just looking at the shape of a person's face and their features and just know what will look best for them. She says he is very rarely wrong. It is because of his deep caring that people follow him from salon to salon and bring their children and their friends to him.

A Second Love

During his college years, Leon was visiting a friend who was hospitalized. When he left the hospital, he thought he noticed a man following behind him. Doubting it at first, he became more sure of it when he had walked several miles with this stranger still in his wake. Deciding it would be best to confront the man in the open where there were lots of people, he spun on his heel, walked straight up to him and simply asked outright if he was following him. To his surprise, the man laughed as he confirmed that he had indeed been following Leon all the way from the hospital. His laughter was disarming and Leon found himself laughing as well. "My name is Terry. Let me buy you coffee" he said, and that was the start of a wonderful forty-five-year life partner relationship. Funny thing is, Leon doesn't normally even drink coffee!

Though this story is not about Leon's relationship with Terry, it's hard to write anything about Leon without at least mentioning Terry. Friends say that Terry was like the other half of Leon's Being. They complemented each other in every aspect of their living, and you would be hard pressed to find a happier couple.

Terry was truly the other passion in Leon's life besides hairdressing. He always wondered how he was so lucky to have this well-educated, charming man as his life partner for so many years. Terry was taken from him in June of 2009. Though he mourns his passing and misses him every day, he still gives thanks to God for the years that they enjoyed together.

Postscript

Leon has felt a presence looking over him, keeping him safe and sane ever since the time of the accident which took the life of his mother and two siblings when he was called to be somewhere else. He lives in gratitude for those people who have been there for him ever since. He feels like he has been guided to them by an invisible hand ever present in his life. There have been those like the fellow hitchhiker, the old couple he worked with at Mosenthals, and the friends who invited him to live with them in Bancroft who seem to be there to help him avoid trouble. Then there are those like every boss he has had who helped him advance his education and thrive in the work that he loves. In fact, he says that there seems to have been hundreds of people in his life who have shown him kindness. Foremost among them was Terry who supported him in every thing that he did.

Nearing the end of his seventh decade now, Leon is still serving people. He knows that God blessed him the day that sixteen-year-old boy was led to an "Apprentice Wanted" sign in a hairdresser's window in Zimbabwe. There is a mutual love and respect between Leon and his clients. At least 10% of them, like Louise, come from across Joburg or even from neighboring towns to have him do their hair. If you're ever in Johannesburg and in need of a haircut, you might want to seek him out.

INTRODUCTION TO "TELLING STORIES"

Some people have really big dreams that don't seem to match their physical stature. I'm sure there weren't many people telling Muggsy Bogues that the 5'3" basketball player should set his sights on the NBA. Bogues, however, had a big dream, and he fulfilled it. Not only did he play fifteen years in the NBA and have a sterling career, he even blocked a shot once from the 7-foot tall Patrick Ewing!

When you are barely 5' tall, weigh less than 100 pounds, and have your sights set on telling stories, that's not so surprising. Many people would encourage you to follow your bliss and be a writer. When you then tell them that you would prefer carrying around 65 pounds of gear and travel to the far reaches of third world countries to tell those stories, THEN you might be met with some skepticism. Really - who would do such a thing? Meet Alicia Sully................

TELLING STORIES

I first met Alicia in Philadelphia in September of 2007. She and I and 46 other Peace Corps Trainees (that's what you are called before you complete two months of training and become Peace Corps Volunteers) were participating in two days of training before getting on a big bird headed for Ghana, West Africa. Actually, it wasn't exactly training. It was more like the Peace Corps trying to convince all of us that we really didn't want to do this. I think it was meant to shake out any fence-sitters before the US Government paid good money to ship us to Africa. They should have tried harder because a few had tickets for a government-paid trip back to the U.S. within two months, but that's another story. Alicia and I stayed.

I didn't take a poll, but I would guess that 47 of us went over with the idea of helping people in a third world country, having an adventure, making our resumes for work or grad school look good (that would not include me since I was 60 years old) or some combination of those reasons. Some of us (or at least I) weren't sure why we were there. Alicia knew exactly why she was there. She was there to tell stories.

"The world needs more story-telling and there just aren't many story-tellers," Alicia told me. Her favorite way of telling stories is through films. By 2015, she had done films to tell stories about camel milk, unsung African heroes, cooking, solar-powered and windmill-powered irrigation, Congolese refugees, and a raft of other topics. She had done films to tell stories in the U.S., Ghana, Kenya, Papua New Guinea, Lebanon, Rawanda, Haiti, and Somaliland. She will likely end up visiting most of the countries in the U.N. before she's done. But I'm getting ahead of myself. Let's back up a decade or so before that meeting in Philadelphia.

Igniting the Flame

Alicia loved stories from the time she was a little girl. She wanted to be a writer or maybe a detective, whose job was to put together the clues to tell the story of what had happened. By the time she reached puberty, she had discovered that she had talents in writing, art, and technical "stuff," all of the skills needed to make films. Maybe film could be her story-telling vehicle. To see if this was really "her thing," she took a video class; and the fuse was lit.

She continued taking classes at a local cable company and was by far the youngest person in those classes. As part of the class, she did her first real film project. It was simply filming a waitress in a diner. That, plus some fun little things she had done with her friends, gave her enough experience to create a resume.

Receiving her certification before reaching the age of fifteen, she was hired to do some production work on cooking and talk shows on TV. Then came an opportunity to work with a team filming a pro-life project. It was incredibly exciting to work on a "real" film, but it felt a little weird for Alicia since it wasn't in alignment with her personal beliefs. This great film-making experience introduced her to the ethical question of whether she would work on projects not in line with her personal outlook on life. This was a question that would come up again later in her professional career.

Choosing a Focus

Alicia was hooked. Her career path was established. Telling stories through film had become her passion at a very young age. The question was, which stories should she tell? Businesses have one type of story to tell people about their companies and another type of story to sell their products. Families have stories to tell through weddings, bar mitzvahs, and other major life events. Charities have stories to tell about their causes. Governments have stories to tell about their policies. There are stories for education, entertainment, commerce, travel and politics. Where should she focus her time and energy?

Part of the answer to that question was hidden in her DNA.

Alicia's parents were anthropologists who had lived in the tiny African country of Swaziland and nearby Botswana. Her dad, Paul Sully, was a "proper hippie" who had been to Woodstock and registered as a conscientious objector when drafted during the Viet Nam war. When he returned from Peace Corps stints in Colombia and Liberia, he attended grad school at the State University of New York (SUNY), Buffalo, where he met Diane Gardsbane. Like him, she was anti-government, as were so many young people in the 60's. Still, he convinced her that the Peace Corps, though part of the US Government, was a worthwhile thing to do. Upon graduation, she joined and was sent to Swaziland. He joined her toward the end of her two year Peace Corps service.

They traveled Africa together, making a film documenting the process of becoming a sacred healer within different cultures. He handled the filming while she captured the sound. They loved traveling to exotic places, particularly in Africa. When Diane became pregnant with Alicia, however, they realized that the amount of work necessary to raise a family would require a return to Louisiana where Diane's parents could help out.

During her childhood, Alicia got to watch her parents' African documentary, which had been donated to the Smithsonian Museum. It captured her imagination. When school was out during the summers, she traveled with her parents to Mexico, Alaska, and other locations on their anthropology trips. Alicia discovered that she shared her parents' love for travel and studying other cultures. When she was eight years old, she accompanied her dad on a trip to Morocco and Spain and was shocked to see that restaurants had no ice to put into drinks. This was her first realization that living conditions were different in other parts of the world than they were in the U.S.

Her awareness of a wider world increased as her "Uncle Joe" came to visit them several times. This man, befriended by Paul when he was serving with the Peace Corps in Liberia, had gone on to become Vice President of that country. Years later, Alicia would stay with Uncle Joe several times when visiting his country.

With her inherited love for travel and exploring other cultures, Alicia set her sights on telling stories of the third world.

Getting to Africa

While choosing a major for college may have been a question mark for many students, it was a no-brainer for Alicia. Yet, she came close to dropping her formal education in film after just two years. One of her classmates, Brad, convinced her that they could learn a lot more by simply making films. The plan, such as it was, was to travel around the country in a remodeled ambulance he planned to buy and shoot whatever they thought was interesting. Breaking off an existing relationship, Alicia opted to become partners with Brad. When their personal relationship fell apart, she stayed at the University of New York at Purchase where she got her Bachelor of Fine Arts degree. Brad went touring the country to make films. Her time with Brad, though short-lived, was critical to her future as it helped her assess what she wanted from life. It was this experience that set the course for her independent approach to story-telling that has defined her ever since those early days.

Following the path of most struggling college students, Alicia found work where she could. The night shift at a coffee shop was where she learned the invaluable skill of making "real" cappuccino. This job only lasted until she found someone on Craig's List who wanted to make a documentary about his life. The twist that captured her was that he wanted the story told from the perspective of his Jack Russell Terrier. Talk about an interesting subject! This man claimed he had been recruited by the FBI/CIA to consult on propaganda work in Haiti and the Dominican Republic. He said that it was quite a lucrative job, and he had gotten accustomed to living the high life with the gorgeous women and fast cars seen in the James Bond films. He also hinted that he had done some "really bad things" in his life, and he suffered severely from bi-polar disorder. He assured her that he had that condition under control with a new medication.

Experiencing more fascination than fear and seeing the opportunity to make much more money than in the coffee shop, Alicia took the job. She spent hours with this man. Mostly they would sit around, talk, and get stoned. Though she never finished that project, she was paid well and racked up many hours of experience shooting film. In effect, it launched her career.

Upon graduation, Alicia followed in her parent's footsteps, joining the Peace Corps (PC). It was perfect for her, putting her right where she wanted to be — in a small village in Ghana, listening to people's stories. Limited to 80 pounds of luggage by Peace Corps regulations, she may have left a lot of things on the PC checklist home, but her camera equipment was carefully packed and went with her.

The first thing you tend to notice about Alicia is that she is outweighed by the camera equipment she is carrying around. Well, maybe not quite, but at 97 pounds, it is no mean feat to haul around what can be 65 pounds on her back! Nevertheless, she wouldn't go anywhere without it.

Not waiting for an assignment, Alicia began shooting films in the village of Forikrom where she lived during our eight week PC training period. She even filmed some of our training activities. There may have been a time when I saw Alicia without her camera, but I can't bring it to mind. One of our Ghanaian instructors suggested that Alicia do a film on Kayayo.

Every year, there is a massive migration of women and young girls from Ghana's poorer, rural north to the southern urban areas. Known as Kayayo, some of these women get work carrying heavy loads on their heads. The work is hard and the pay is small. You see them sleeping on the streets, and many are lured into sexual slavery in exchange for shelter. This was exactly the kind of story that Alicia would love to tell in order to bring awareness to village women before they entered into this trap.

That project almost ended before it started. Alicia quickly found out that this was a taboo subject. It was almost impossible to find anyone that would talk to her about it. Mohammed saved her. Each Peace Corps Volunteer (PCV) is assigned a "counterpart" in the village s/he goes to. This is both their business and social liaison to the village. Let's just say that some counterparts are better than others. Mohammed was a shining star. He was everything Alicia could possibly ask for: artistic, technical, and easy to work with. He quickly became her best friend, collaborator, and source of inspiration. With his help, she began to find people who were willing to speak with her about Kayayo. When they understood her intention, she was able to put together a "cast," though none had ever acted, and make a professional film. Having seen this film myself, I can tell you that Alicia is a magician to have created this story with no resources, no professional team, no money, and working with village people who had never done any acting. It really is a good film that tells the tale well. Though the entire film was not available on line at the time of this writing, you can pull up "Kayayo - Part 1" and "Kayayo - Part 2" on YouTube to get portions of it.

She toured many villages in northern Ghana, setting up her equipment in the dirt and showing the film on a sheet or whatever else could be improvised. Though there are no statistics on how many women were saved the horrors of Kayayo, she was well received everywhere she went; and the message got out. You can learn a bit about the tour that Alicia took with fellow film-maker Peter Campo at https://vimeo.com/9587924.

She had now followed the trail blazed by her parents and created a meaningful documentary film telling one of Africa's many stories.

Life After Peace Corps

Alicia was "excused" from the Peace Corps in the Fall of 2009 having completed 25 of the 27 month commitment. Though she was doing an excellent job, she was caught riding a motorcycle, a one-strike-you're-out offense. They paid her ticket back to the U.S., but Africa was now in her blood; and her video career was off and running.

She had started a project for a mango company, ITFC, while still in the PC. The company wanted this film to show the mango business through all four seasons; so, after only three weeks at home in the U.S., Alicia returned to Ghana as an ITFC employee to finish the project.

Then came the Unsung Heroes of Africa project, the brain-child of Sebastian, another man she had met while she was in the Peace Corps. (Who knew that her PC contacts would become such an integral part of her professional life?) He knew the story he wanted to tell and needed a film-maker to shoot it. Right up Alicia's alley! This ambitious project took almost three months and included filming in Ghana, Morocco, Mauritania, Angola, Namibia, South Africa, Cameroon, Burkina Faso, Mali, Western Sahara, Senegal, Nigeria, Republic of the Congo, and the Democratic Republic of the Congo, as well as busing through Togo and Benin. To make the trip financially viable they would shoot stories in each location that were contracted by a local individual or organization. Later, they would edit together pieces from each locale to create their larger project.

Starting with just three people crazy about making films, the company evolved over six years into a team of eleven people — eleven very talented and very flexible people. Everyone on the team can film, edit, write, produce and whatever else it takes to complete a job. The number of people working on any given project depends on the scope and complexity of that film.

The African Heroes concept was embraced by a Non-Governmental Organization (NGO) operating in Papua New Guinea (PNG). They agreed to fund a similar project there. As a result, Alicia found herself meeting Sebastian and a crew in Hong Kong a few months after finishing their Africa project, and off they went to PNG. Finding that the "heroes" they were planning to glorify were actually quite corrupt, they shifted gears to do a story about beetle nuts. Alicia found that she loved telling "food" stories as long as they were original and had real value to people. From this passion came the Camel milk/cheese project.

Being a cheese lover, this was a natural for Alicia. Working on the camel milk project, she traveled to eighteen of the 100 countries where camel milk was sold. As she learned about its nutritional value, she was astounded to find that it was used as medicine to treat autism, heart disease, diabetes, and a wide variety of other ailments. Alicia even did a ten day camel milk detox herself and saw how healthy and energized she felt as a result. She realized that this was, indeed, a superfood. Even though camel milk is available almost everywhere from camel farms or online, knowledge of it was limited to those who lived with camels. She was determined to educate the people who could benefit the most, so she made a few different films. In addition to a film for camel conferences (yes - there really ARE camel conferences!), she posted a film on the web through her own channel, did TEDxtalks (search for "camel milk" on www.tedxtalks.tedx.com), and even created a documentary. She also shared it on Mongolian TV to get the word out across the country. Camels only thrive in one area of Mongolia, but people throughout the country could benefit hugely from the milk. She is currently working on a version for film festivals and, hopefully, larger distribution. Needless to say, she LOVES camel milk.

Choosing Projects

The camel milk / cheese story is a good example of a project that simply caught her interest as a fascinating story to tell. Though she may not get paid by a sponsor for stories like this, she loves doing them. They also build her portfolio, and she makes many connections during the filming that help her find paying jobs. Alicia has found kindred souls through Kickstarter (an online fund-raising organization). They believe enough in what she is doing, even though they've never met her, that she raised $8000 for the camel milk project and $6000 for the African Heroes project. In addition, she usually finds that people in the villages to which she travels will provide her accommodations for free.

Of course, she couldn't feed her story-telling habit without paying gigs. She and her partners approach organizations that interest them to see if the company might find value in having their story effectively told. Alicia's combination of high quality, fair price, and extreme creativity lead to proliferating work. From one job that she did in Liberia, four more were born in that country in 2011 alone.

As she learned at a young age, there are times when there is a story to be told that is not compatible with her personal beliefs. Alicia says that she would not enter into a project that she couldn't be proud of, but there are times when she doesn't understand the scope or direction of a project until they are well into it. In cases where they don't feel good about a project, they will finish it and provide it to the client but will not promote it or post it on their site. One example, in international development work, is "poverty porn." This is a term used to describe a piece that skews the facts to make people look worse off than they really are in order to elicit sympathy from the intended market. She did a story on a solar lamp project for Congolese refugees in Rwanda. The organization didn't think their fund-raiser would be successful showing the men wearing suits and hats, as is their custom, so they had her focus instead on children playing in the dirt.

Hired to do a story on solar- and windmill-powered irrigation, she found out that the project was a sham. The pipes had burst and people would spin the windmill by hand to make it look like it was working. She reported the facts to the company who had contracted with her, but they had her shoot the story anyway since they were so deeply invested in it.

The Process

Most of Alicia's work involves shooting real people in their normal lives. The first step is getting to know them and their environment, which usually entails living with them. This can be a bit tricky. If she gets too close to them, she can end up with too many ideas for too many stories about too many people! She strives to be invisible and go unnoticed — not an easy task for a white woman usually in a village of black or brown people. Whenever possible, she makes an early contact with someone in the village. Being introduced to those whom she intends to film by a local person increases the trust factor significantly.

There are times when previous experience with camera crews have left local people distrustful. Such was the case for a project she was hired to do about Chef Jose Andres in Haiti. Alicia and her crew took the time to shoot some scenes that were fun and light. When they showed these to the people involved, it won them over and things went smoothly from there.

The initial steps, getting to know the people and doing the filming, are Alicia's favorite part of the process. That's where the fun is! Editing — not so much. It can be tiring, frustrating work and,if a piece is just not coming together, may entail working all night. Still, she can't always convince another member of the team to take on the editing process. When a project finally does come out perfect, she says it is better than sex or chocolate.

There are occasions, such as a Somaliland Peace Building project, where she is hired to do the story when the event has already been completed.

This was a fascinating piece involving a consortium of three large NGOs that were helping a community apply for grants and put together a plan for what they would do with the money. By the time Alicia was hired, they had already finished leading the parties involved through the community mapping process (determining what needs would be filled, the role of the community, and the resources needed) and had applied for the grants. This was called a "peace building" project because the factions of the community that were involved did not get along. Tensions were often high, and navigating the emotions was as important to the project as putting together the plan. To effectively capture this on film, Alicia and her team had to work with all parties involved to re-enact parts of the entire process!

Though most projects are fairly limited in time, some, like the camel milk project, can last a year or more. Actual filming time generally ranges from five days to several weeks, and longer projects may require multiple videos and several locations. One job involved filming in New York, Denmark, Rwanda, Lebanon and Sri Lanka. Those six weeks of shooting yielded two videos totaling six minutes! Since each job has its own scope of work, it is very rare that all eleven people would be needed on a single job, so there are always multiple projects happening simultaneously. In fact, a specific person might be doing the writing for one job, editing another, shooting a third, and working on a proposal for a fourth. Nobody on the team gets bored!

The Challenges

As a "tech nomad," Alicia lives out of a backpack, interacting with her closet only on occasion. She has to pack light yet prepare for everything — different climates, professional clothes and trekking clothes. On a recent trip, she needed clothes to withstand a Washington, D.C. blizzard while also accounting for the blistering heat of Haiti. She usually ends up with a clothing backpack of thirty pounds to go with the thirty-five pound equipment backpack which she will not trust to airport luggage handlers. There is also her tripod and jib (mini-crane). It is when she gets off the plane and heads to remote areas using questionable public transportation on roads that resemble a pothole collection that carting all of this stuff around is a real test for her ninety-seven pound body. She is quite a sight with her equipment backpack and tripod on her back, the clothes pack worn in front and a small bag over her shoulder!

She loves this life that she's been living since 2009 but admits that it is not for everybody. It can certainly put a strain on a marriage. When she first married Pedro in 2012, it seemed like a match made in heaven since he loved what she loved. When they couldn't find agreement on the team she had put together, however, he started his own company. They no longer work together and often don't see each other for weeks at a time. So far, it's working for both of them, especially the honeymoon atmosphere created each time they come back together.

Having shot footage in more than 70 countries, Alicia has found that immigration security at the borders can be a sticky situation. Since they have no work visas, they enter each country as tourists. Many an immigration official has wondered what kind of tourist carries all of this movie equipment. They were interrogated by ten agents for forty-five minutes once at the Kenya/Uganda border including reviewing what was on all of their computers. Alicia believes it was a *nun* sitting next to her on the bus who had turned them in after seeing some footage of Somalis that they were editing. The tension at the time between Uganda and Somalia created the suspicion.

At times, they have to shoot from the hip and hope to get lucky. They couldn't get an Angola visa for longer than four days. Knowing it was going to be very difficult, if not impossible, to finish the job in that length of time, they decided to go for it anyway. During the process of the shoot, they happened to meet just the right people who knew how to get them extensions so they could do the job properly. In other countries, they found that the only way to get the proper visas involved a blank envelope with the right amount of money in it handed to just the right person at the border.

Uzbekistan is a police state that doesn't allow media. In 2011, Alicia had gone in to do a bit of the camel milk story and only took a DSLR photo camera, which also does video, in order to avoid suspicion. When the family the crew was staying with noticed a BBC pen Alicia had, they called the police. Suddenly, Alicia and her cohorts were like Jason Bourne, running and barely catching a train before they were apprehended. Had they been caught, they would surely have been jailed.

Even something as simple as food can be a problem. In many countries, they have no way to get any more money. If the job takes longer than expected, they run out of food money. Though not as big a problem for Alicia, larger members of the crew require more calories. A 6'9" member of her crew got very sick and weak on a shoot. They simply could not get him the calories he needed.

When food is available, it is often limited to rice, pasta and other starches with little protein available. Since discovering the benefits of camel milk, Alicia looks for it wherever they travel to provide the nutrition they need. Flying as much as she does, she has become a "Gold" member of Star Alliance. The employees in the Star Alliance lounge in Switzerland must wonder why the tiny woman with the camera equipment stuffs her pockets with the wrapped cheeses they have available for snacks! Those cheese snacks helped keep her crew alive on a Swaziland trip where food was scarce.

The Muslim countries they work in tend to be a bit safer than others but security must always be considered in every country. Equipment can easily disappear whether they are in Nairobi (known as "Nai-robbery") or a small rural village. Alicia lost a sound recorder to a pick-pocket on a bus, and once someone tried to snatch her cell phone out of her hand while she was sitting in a taxi. That would have been the second cell phone stolen. Now crew members all lock the doors and close taxi windows when they need to make a call. When on location, one crew member is assigned to watch the equipment. Cameras are not casually put down, but rather replaced in a zip-able bag when not in use.

Many film locations have no hotels, so getting accommodations is another tricky factor. Though rural people tend to be very gracious, Alicia has found that the "Three Day Rule" usually applies. You will be accepted as an honored guest for that length of time, and then cultural awareness bids you to move on. If she is doing a solo shoot, she sometimes finds that her bond with the family results in an invitation for her to stay longer, but this rarely applies when a whole crew is involved.

Housing can often be arranged ahead of time for short projects, especially in places where they have previously visited. Long projects, like the camel milk story, are so unpredictable and they have to move so often, that they simply have to show up and ask around to see who is willing to house them.

When a group of people are all doing something that they love, money is never the primary concern. Still, everybody does like to eat, so it has to be addressed. The first few years, when there were only three people on the team, they were like a traveling commune, pooling everyone's money to pay for expenses, travel, food and equipment. There was no "personal" money. As the team grew, the system broke down. People actually wanted to have a life! Since everyone is a full-time contractor, the challenge was coming up with a fair way to pay everybody. They settled on a system of a percentage of the project income, minus expenses, based on whether the individual had done shooting, editing, production, writing etc. Not everyone worked on every project, and the most enjoyable projects were usually the ones with the lowest budget. As a result each team member had to strike a balance between fun and income.

Traveling in third-world countries using local transportation, limited food, and often working long hours has its health hazards so insurance is also an issue. Alicia is still working on this one.

Communication has been, shall we say, most interesting. In Kenya alone, there are 52 languages; and in Ghana, over 70! Transcription is challenging enough in English, as is editing. Transcribing and editing one interview to get a concise, intelligent end product could easily take hours. It is even more difficult when the final video is to be in a language unknown to the film-makers. This requires a translator. Since professional translators are as rare in rural areas as the Abominable Snowman, the person they end up with may speak very limited English. They may even just get up and leave halfway through a story because they have some place else to go or simply get tired. The flip side is almost as bad. When you are required to have everyone speak English for a film, the people you are interviewing will not be able to go into depth in a language in which they are not well-versed.

The answer to this dilemma is to train a translator, but this takes a long time and is only practical in a country where they do multiple stories. Such a place is Somalia. Alicia took the time to train a translator there which made it possible for them to accept an assignment to do a story entirely in Somali. Possible, yes, but far from easy! Having come close to quitting once, things got even tougher when Alicia and her crew were forced to leave

Somalia for security reasons. Now all they had to do was finish a film made in Somalia, in Somali, for Somalians without being there or speaking the language! Explaining her dilemma to her clients, she gave them the option to back out of the contract and find someone else to make the film. Such is Alicia's reputation that the client gave her a vote of confidence and stayed with her. Sub-contracting portions to a local Somali film company, she found a way to finish the job so that the client was well satisfied; and Alicia was happy with the final product — exhausted, but happy.

Alicia accepts all of these challenges as simply part of what she has chosen to do with her life. She loves the fact that she can go anywhere in the world and find a story to tell that people will want to hear. She is addicted to experiencing new cultures. She has even found fascinating sub-cultures present in the U.S. Such is the Burning Man Festival she shot in 2014 — an entire village of tens of thousands of people gathered in Nevada's Black Rock Desert. This is a huge, but temporary, metropolis dedicated to community, art, self-expression, and self-reliance.

PostScript

As of the writing of this story, Alicia is working on a US version of the camel milk documentary, various UN projects to pay the bills, a sailing/film project, and more experimental social impact work. Just as important, she is finding ways to spend more time with Pedro.

To learn more about Alicia and her team, go to www.whattookyousolong.org

INTRODUCTION TO "THE BANKER TURNED PHOTOGRAPHER"

Some people hate their jobs. Some people love their jobs. Some people really like their jobs, but their passion lies somewhere else. The people in this last category have the most difficult challenge. If you hate your job, then it's really not that hard to quit and follow your passion; but it's not that easy when you really like your job and you are making a good living. Those people have a few choices:

1. Give up your passion - not a good choice as it might feed the body but kill the soul.
2. Give up your job and follow your passion - a good choice for some people but not an easy one to make.
3. Follow your passion in your non-work time - also a good choice for some people but it leaves little time for family and other pursuits.

Hmmm.....what to do? What to do?

The perfect solution might be to do the work you really like for 30 years and then let that pension finance your passion full-time after that. Even better would be if you could find a way to weave your passion into situations where your work takes you during those 30 years. But, come on, who could work that out? Meet Colin Mead........

THE BANKER TURNED PHOTOGRAPHER

I met Colin Mead and his wife Margaret at the Bryanston Organic Market while I was visiting South Africa in 2013. His physical presence speaks of a quiet, unassuming man who could easily be a model for a kindly grandfather. The photos hanging in his booth, all of which he took himself, speak of an adventurer, a daring world traveler with a sharp eye for the dramatic and artistic. I doubt if Colin would describe himself as an adventurer but what else would you call a man who has travelled from South Africa to the U.S., Europe, Canada, South America, and Antarctica, not to mention Botswana, Namibia, Uganda, Tanzania and many other countries in Africa just to take photos of some of the most beautiful, and dangerous animals and landscapes in the world?

When you see the body and the scope of his work, it's hard to believe that photography first became his career in 1995 at 55 years of age.

Born in Cardiff, Wales, Colin lived in England in his early years. On his eighth birthday, his father presented him with a simple box camera, a Brownie. There began his passion for photography. Colin carried that box camera everywhere he went and took pictures of everything that interested him.

This passion kicked up a notch at ten years of age. At that time, his father, a Minister of Religion in the Salvation Army, accepted a position in Salisbury, Rhodesia (now Harare, Zimbabwe) and then, two years later, was appointed to a position in Johannesburg, South Africa. Colin very quickly fell in love with the wild beauty and enormous diversity of wildlife in Africa. He had truly found home.

Another love of his was travel, and this was encouraged by his parents. When he was fifteen years old, with his beloved thirteen-year-old sister in tow, he hitchhiked from Johannesburg, South Africa to Kenya, East Africa and back, a total of 5500 km (3400 miles). This would be like going from New York to San Francisco and almost half way back again. They were gone about a month, and Colin almost wore out his box camera taking pictures of it all. This was the first of several trips with his sister, including a jaunt to Europe.

When Colin was seventeen, his dad, a scoutmaster with the Boy Scouts, led a group of 400 South African scouters to the Boy Scout Jubilee Jamboree held in Sutton Coldfield, U.K. Of course, Colin went along and became a Queen's Scout.

At nineteen, with little more than his camera (now a Minolta, a huge improvement over his previous cameras) and a few clothes, Colin set off on a daring photographic expedition. He started by hitchhiking to the bustling port city of Durban and simply walked around the docks taking pictures and making contacts there. Before long he found work on a merchant vessel. Colin continued to work passage on ships which would take him, more than once, around the world.

Two years later, as a twenty-one-year-old seasoned photographer, Colin returned to South Africa deeply inspired to continue to capture on film the intense beauty he had witnessed throughout God's creation.

Landing in Cape Town on his return voyage, he discovered what was to become another deep passion in his life - Margaret. Active in the Cape Town Salvation Army, she later left her family and moved up to Johannesburg, worshipping at the same church where Colin played in the Salvation Army brass band. He remembered her from Cape Town and they renewed their relationship, which led to marriage. They have now been loving partners for more than fifty years.

Blending Passion With Making a Living

As much as Colin loved photography, he couldn't see how he could make a living from it so when he left school, he went to work for a large bank in South Africa. He next worked for one of the national discount houses, and later a large mining house, which handled billions of dollars in funds in the mining and financial sectors. He continued in this sector for more than thirty years.

Though he enjoyed his career a great deal, photography continued to fill his heart. Fortunately, he didn't have to sacrifice one for the other. A huge perk of his career was that it gave him opportunity to travel to the U.S., Canada, Australia, New Zealand, Europe, and other parts of Africa to study their financial markets. His camera was always the first thing to be packed on these trips, and he took advantage of spare time to explore the natural wonders that each country had to offer.

Earning a very good living, he used the leave time he was allowed to further his travels around the world, many times with his wife and his beloved Canon camera.

I'm sure you won't be surprised to learn that Colin had built a dark room in his house during his years as a banker. Nor would you be shocked to know that he was a very active member of the Johannesburg Photographic Society (JPS) which met once a month. He became chairman of that organization in his late twenties and remained so for fourteen years. One of his volunteer jobs with the JPS was to organize outings to exotic places like East and Central Africa and the Namib Desert in Namibia, one of the driest deserts in the world and perhaps the only place where a photographer could shoot incredibly beautiful, uniquely-shaped orange and black sand dunes that reach 400 meters high.

Then the magical day came. To keep his pension, he had to work for the Mining House until at least 55 years of age. As much as he enjoyed his banking career, he retired exactly on his 55th birthday and officially launched his second career. At first, he simply went on his own to get pictures he could publish. He created several books containing between 150-200 photos each and also sold individual prints.

The Safaris

After several years, he expanded into doing photographic safaris in South Africa, then East Africa and later, Antarctica, which he visited three times. On these safaris, he not only exposes participants to scenes and wildlife they would otherwise never have seen, but he also teaches them the art of nature photography. In his "practical classroom" with an intimate group of only six people, Colin shows them how to get the best exposures, depth of field, composition, and other elements of photography. They shoot from open safari vehicles, boats on rivers, and tripods on land. He teaches them how to create a human tripod by tucking their elbows into their stomachs to get good shots from the vehicle.

Colin says that, for him, the most critical elements in getting a good picture are composition, patience, and an understanding wife. The latter is critical as he may wait days to get the shot he seeks and Margaret supports him 100%. He once waited in one spot for ten hours to get a shot of a black-backed jackal regurgitating her food to feed her six pups (number 63 on his website photo gallery if you'd like to see the result).

Colin wouldn't live anywhere else in the world, as, in his opinion, the countries of Southern and Equatorial Africa boast a greater abundance of animals and birds than does any other location. On these safaris, they invariably spot lions, leopards, and cheetahs along with giraffes, zebras, and other more common wildlife. Unlike large public reserves like Kruger National Park, the private unfenced reserves chosen by Colin in Africa allow the safari vehicle to go off-road and, due to traversing rights arrangements with adjacent neighbors, they even follow animals they are tracking beyond the lodge's boundaries.

Wondering why people choose Colin over other safaris, I read this comment from John Stewart, a man who has been on many safaris: "One cannot compare the experience of these safaris with any other, as the Rangers are often able to get within a few meters of elephant, rhino, lion, buffalo as well as wild dog, cheetah and more….the drives are always stress free, no juggling for close-ups or for the best positioning of vehicles that almost always occurs in places like [the public parks]. We spend as much time with each specie as we need and quite regularly follow them off the road, as they stalk their prey or just waltz through the bush looking for a high tree to sleep in."

Colin seats one participant next to the driver with the tracker sitting on the front fender. The other six people, including Colin (or the leader of the group,) sit in three rows of 2 people so everyone has a "window" seat. Of course, in the open vehicle there are no windows and views are totally unobstructed. Each row has a middle seat which is used for camera equipment, giving everyone freedom of movement. The leader sits in the second row allowing him to easily pass comments from the driver/tracker to the guests and questions from the guests to the driver/tracker. The expertise of the safari team means there will be little wasted time.

The tracker will "read" the spoor and may say, "There has been a leopard here within 1/2 hour, and he went in that direction." The driver knows the terrain so well that he can make a judgment if it makes sense to proceed in that direction without having to drive into a dead end.

Is it dangerous? Well - being close to wild animals in their own territory always carries a risk, but, along with his professional guides and trackers, Colin has learned to judge each situation for safety. Though animals often "mock charge" the vehicle, it is simply to let them know that they are close enough. He has never had an animal actually come all the way to the vehicle.

The Bottom of the World

Though Africa is his primary joy, in recent years, Colin has also loved to open people to the wonders of Antarctica - for most people, a once in a lifetime thrill. Being a much bigger undertaking, he has only led this safari three times since 2007.

The group, comprising between 7-12 people, first flies to Buenos Aries, Argentina where the travelers spend a couple of days sightseeing. Then they fly to Ushuaia, the southernmost town in the world, in the Argentine province of Tierra del Fuego. They spend a couple of days there before boarding ship and joining other passengers steaming off to the Antarctic continent and surrounding islands, where the ship stops off from time to time, allowing passengers to disembark.

On board the ship, experts lecture on the wildlife of Antarctica and the history of the Antarctic, including explorations dating back 300-500 years. Arriving at the coldest, windiest, driest continent on earth, passengers need to sleep on the ship since there are no accommodations whatsoever on the Antarctic continent. Once they disembark, Colin leads them on a photographic exploration for four hours. Then the group returns to the ship for lunch as the Captain continues 2-3 hours along the coast to deposit them at another location for more photo opportunities.

Though there are zero permanent residents on this entire continent, there are millions of penguins, ideally suited to local conditions. Of the seventeen species of penguins in the world, seven are considered Antarctic penguins with four species living/nesting on the mainland. Being very curious and friendly with no fear of humans, hundreds or even thousands of them surround the people in the group, often pecking at their Wellington boots while being filmed. They love posing for portrait shots so everyone goes home with beautiful and plentiful penguin pictures. To supplement the photo albums, there are incredible opportunities to shoot majestic icebergs, beaches, many other bird varieties, mountains, and even a couple of volcanoes. Though these are considered active, Colin leads his groups to the top edge from which they get magnificent pictures of the crater. The group spends 10-12 days like that and nobody ever tires of it.

Postscript

At 75 years old, Colin is still deeply passionate about two things - his wife Margaret and photography. Go to his website, www.colinmead.co.za and you can see the images that put him on a photographic career path. The first picture on the website photo gallery is still one of his favorites. Fittingly, it is picture #001 in his website photo gallery: a silhouette of an elephant at a still river bank in Northern Botswana during sunset. He had to go there three nights in a row to get this shot. On the second night, there were fifty elephants there. Though it was an incredible sight, it was not the shot he wanted. His reward came the next night when a solitary pachyderm showed up for a drink. I think you'll agree it was worth the wait.

For those serious about photographing nature, Colin and a friend still do between 10 and 12 photographic safaris per year in South Africa - usually to the Madikwe Reserve close to the Botswana border or Timbavati, home of the regal white lion, close to the Mozambique border. Both camps are very comfortable with great food. He guarantees you won't go home hungry! His email contact information is colin@colinmead.co.za.

If, like me, you're not the type to trek after lions, elephants, cheetahs, and other amazing animals on one of Colin's safaris, then simply stop by the Bryanston Organic Market in Johannesburg any Thursday or Saturday between 9am and 3 pm. You'll find Colin and Margaret in Stall 62, as they have been for over thirty years. From mid-November until Christmas there are also Moonlight and Christmas markets between 5 and 9 p.m. Be prepared to make tough choices as I couldn't find a single picture that didn't captivate me.

INTRODUCTION OF
"HOUSES OF HEALING"

Most of us would like to live our whole lives without spending any time in prison. Seems reasonable enough. But what if Life tells you that prison is where you will find your purpose, your fulfillment, your passion? What if you discovered that all of your education, personal experience, and work history was really just preparation for working with inmates? What if you just knew, deep inside your heart, that the only place for you to find meaning in life was inside prison walls? Who would voluntarily commit themselves to prison? Meet Pris.....

HOUSES OF HEALING

In 1995, Pris was 50 years old and perhaps happier than most people. After a troublesome first marriage, she had found Bob, the love of her life, and after twelve years with him, she felt like she had hit the relationship jackpot. Her private practice, as a clinical social worker, had allowed her to help people overcome addictions. In this way, she felt like she was contributing to the world. She hadn't spent a lot of time thinking about any great thing that she was put on this earth to accomplish. Hadn't thought that maybe there was a passion within her soul that was as yet undiscovered so she wasn't really searching.

That year, three different people in totally separate circumstances talked of their work in the prison system. Though she thought that sounded interesting, she took no action and didn't really see it as "her thing." She was not a teacher and didn't work with groups. All that turned around during fifteen minutes in the midst of an eight hour Joan Borysenko workshop that was part of a three day "Body and Soul" program in Boston. Joan was on the board of the Lionheart Foundation, a non-profit, sponsoring, among other things, the distribution of a book called *Houses of Healing.* This was the basis of a thirteen week program designed to help prison inmates turn their lives around. As wonderful as Dr. Borysenko and the rest of the presenters that weekend were, everything outside of that fifteen minutes was a blur for Pris. A voice in her head, triggered by that brief mention of this prison program, kept telling her, "Time to put your money where your mouth is. This is what you are supposed to be doing."

Soon after arriving home from the weekend, she called Robin Casarjian, author of the book and creator of the *Houses For Healing* program. During their ninety-minute telephone conversation, Robin talked about learning from the works of John Bradshaw, Gerald Jampolsky, and others that Pris had used in her counseling work. She couldn't have felt more in tune with this program. Truly believing that this was her work to do, she asked Robin to send her the book and the training manual. Though it was highly unusual to send the manual before someone had read the book, Robin responded to the passion she heard in Pris's voice and immediately sent her both.

Getting Started

The day she sat down to read the book, she was surprised when Bob came home early. When he told her he was actually a bit later than usual, she realized that she was so engrossed in the material that she had completely lost track of time. There had often been something in the back of her mind telling her that there was another direction for her life to take and now she was sure that she had found it. Having received from Robin a list of others who had been teaching in NJ, she started making phone calls. How hard could it be to get started?

If she had known the answer to that question, she might never had started down this path. Everyone on the list had either stopped teaching the course or had never begun. Every time she thought she found an open door, it slammed in her face. Program directors couldn't see how it could fit into the schedule. Other prison officials, even those compassionate to her efforts, told her this would never work with serious offenders. Two months went by. Then three. Then six. Dozens of contacts turned into dozens of rejections. It seemed like failure really might be an option, but every time Pris thought of quitting, a voice inside her head told her, "No way! This is what your soul's journey is about. You're NOT quitting!" Each "no" that she got came with a possible lead to follow so the trail never quite came to an end. After nine fruitless, frustrating months, she was finally able to connect with a woman in the education department of a women's prison in New Jersey. Looking back at that first class, Pris calls it stilted and robotic, but it got things going. Through that connection, she was put in touch with a wonderful prison chaplain who networked her into a nearby men's prison. The administrators there were far from enthused. Since, however, there was no impact on their budget (Pris volunteered her time and provided all materials), they decided to let her give it a shot, certain that it would have little impact. After all, how many male prisoners were going to jump at the chance to join "group therapy," as they saw it, and "get in touch with their feelings?"

Boy - were they surprised! The program caught on and continued to grow. Today, after over eighteen years, Pris still does one to two nights per week at the men's prison with up to 25 men in each class. She also did two classes per week at the women's prison, one in the maximum-security unit and one on grounds. Those classes were limited to 20 but not for a shortage of willing participants. Pris found that the women were often more emotionally damaged than the men and needed more individual attention so she kept the class size smaller.

The Perfect Fit

Pris originally intended to pursue a career in nursing but dropped out of college to raise a family with her first husband. When the kids were older and she felt the draw to work in the world, she evaluated her strengths to see what might be the best fit. To resume nursing, she felt she would have to start all over again since twenty years had passed. It seemed like people were always telling her what a good listener she was. Many found themselves telling her things that they had never told anyone else, not even their spouse nor closest friends. "You have a way of helping me see how things fit together that clarifies my vision and makes sense of my life," they would tell her. At the time, she felt like she needed clarity in her own life as she was dealing with her husband's drinking problem and contemplating divorce. This led her to a career as a clinical social worker in Syracuse, New York. She started out doing marriage counseling and quickly found out that she hated it! In considering other directions, she realized that her experience living with an alcoholic made her compassionate towards people with addictions as well as those who suffered from anxiety and depression. She deeply understood the issues plaguing addicts and the people who were close to them. Though she did therapy in other areas, this was truly her niche. She enjoyed working with people and helping them make major positive changes in their lives. At the same time, she found it frustrating that real progress was often limited by insurance practices and other outside pressures. It hurt to see people start down a path of recovery and then not get to see it all the way through. She began to wonder if there wasn't a better way to create a higher percentage of success stories. As this question was swirling around in her mind, she and Bob moved to New Jersey, and she was contemplating whether to start up a private practice in her new location. Enter the "Body and Soul" program, Joan Borysenko, and Pris's discovery of the *Houses of Healing* program.

One section of the book deals with the impact of inner child issues on one's adult life. This was something she certainly knew about from personal experience. As she was growing up, how many times had she heard, "What's wrong with you? Why can't you be more like your brother?" She threw temper tantrums up to the age of twelve and developed what she came to know later as a sub-personality based on feeling "not good enough." In nursing school, she would always ask someone else to go first as she was sure that her offering was inadequate. It was when she returned to school many years later and studied social work that she clearly saw how her childhood issues had held her back in many areas of her adult life. Understanding herself was to prove invaluable to her work with prisoners.

Over the ten years she was in practice in Syracuse, she had added skill sets to her toolbox. She had become a Credentialed Addictions Counselor and studied hypnotherapy, meditation, and past-life regression work. In *Houses of Healing*, she found a combination of everything that she had used in her therapy and addiction work in time-limited, organized, teachable sessions. This was a dream come true as she had never come up with a way to organize all that she knew into this type of program. Everything that she had done had brought her to this point, and now she had the perfect tool to manifest meaningful results. In addition, she had discovered a "captive" audience who could make huge changes in their lives - changes that they never thought possible and would not have sought on the "outside."

The Process

The class is voluntary for inmates who first attend an orientation to confirm that it is right for them. This is followed by three weeks where the participants are introduced to meditation and other aspects that will be important in the class work. Pris lets them know that this may seem like the "boring" part of the class, but it is foundational to the deeper work they will be doing. She asks for a commitment to the first four weeks. At the end of this period, some will drop out as they may not be ready to handle the strong emotions that come up with the inner child work that starts in week five. Others may join the class during those first four weeks as they become encouraged by other inmates, but nobody is allowed to join the class after that period. Perhaps the most important part of the first four sessions is that the group develops trust bonds with Pris and with each other. She requests, if possible, that there be no Correctional Officer present during the classes. Each member of the group is sworn to the confidentiality of personally shared information. Anyone breaking that agreement is dropped from the course. Thus, the participants come to accept this as a safe space and relax into it. In the eighteen years that Pris has taught the course, she has not had a single issue with inmate misconduct.

Many inmates have a victim mentality themselves, often nurtured by difficult and abusive childhoods and addictions. They are used to feeling "less than." For this reason, Pris has the group meet in a circle promoting equality. Since some inmates have truly gut-wrenching stories of their childhoods, she emphasizes for others that there are no "minor" issues. She makes it clear that childhood wounding strongly influences adult lives regardless of how much less severe one person's experience seems compared to another.

Small group work, often with just two members to a group, starts right from the beginning. The men and women are often uneasy during those first sessions, feeling uncomfortable answering the question "Who am I really?" with another individual. That discomfort soon disappears and most of them come to truly love the work.

For the purposes of this story, I won't go into much detail on the class content. I would direct those interested to obtain a copy of the book, *Houses of Healing*, available on Amazon or through lionheart.org. I would note that this material would be helpful to everyone, not just inmates, because in many ways we are all prisoners of our own secrets, difficulties and childhood issues. I would like to mention a few points related to the last two weeks of this thirteen week course.

In the twelfth week, Pris takes the class members through a guided relaxation exercise where they walk down a hallway of possibilities. There is a large, cold door on the left side that cannot be opened or might begin to open a crack but then slams shut. This is the door to their past. She explains that the past is over; and they cannot return there, but they can always continue to learn from those experiences. Further down the hall is a doorway of possibilities. In it is a large white board. As they think of something - anything - all they need do is touch the board and that possibility will be automatically written there in bright neon letters. Before leaving, they breathe those possibilities deeply into their mind and bodies. At the end of the hallway is one last door - the door to their future, but they can't enter in there yet. It is locked.

In week thirteen, she takes them through the same exercise, but this time she gives them the key to that last door. She asks them to enter the "room of the future" and to invite anyone else of their choosing to join them. She asks them to celebrate as they see images of what the future might bring. After a while, she asks that they return to the hallway, for one cannot live in the future but only plan for and create it. She reminds them that only *they* now hold the key to their future and that it can unlock that door whenever they choose to do so.

This thirteen week process empowers participants with the essentials of choice as they recognize how drugs, alcohol, and childhood wounds have affected their lives and realize that tomorrow can be quite different from yesterday.

Meet the Graduates

"John" had been kicked down his entire life and always knew that he'd never amount to anything. It was inevitable that his drug dealing would eventually get him into jail. There he met Pris or, as her students called her, Ms. P. For the first time, someone saw him as more than just another worthless junkie. This course was opening his eyes to the fact that he had the power to create a different life for himself — a better life. He couldn't get enough of it. He took copious notes in class and dedicated his time outside of the class to studying. Not once did he miss completing an assignment. When the thirteen weeks ended, he immediately approached Mrs. P. and asked if he would be allowed to take it again! Watching the tremendous growth process transform this twenty-four year old lost little boy into a confident, responsible, caring man was the kind of payment that Pris had longed for and was now receiving in her work. When he finished that second cycle, he was a completely different person, and Pris **knew** that this would be the last time "John" would ever return to prison.

"Tom" had been addicted to heroin since he was ten years old and supported his habit by dealing. He was abandoned by his father at a very early age, and his crack-addicted mother might as well have been absent. When he was high on heroin, his whole life seemed bigger, brighter and so much more alive. It felt like being with the most beautiful, adoring woman in the world, and he went back to her time and again. But he learned she was a "demanding and treacherous mistress." At 20, he was in prison and there he found Pris and her *Houses of Healing* program. On day one, she told him that she would try her best to help him find something that meant more to him than getting high and that would keep him out of prison and help him create a meaningful, productive life. At the end of thirteen magical (yet sometimes frustrating) weeks, he told her that, for the first time in his life, he was beginning to like himself. He realized how much his girlfriend and their four year-old daughter really meant to him and, just as important, how much they truly loved him. Here was a clear path out of his old pattern of abandonment and lack of love. "Tom" finally experienced hope.

These are just two stories of hundreds. Of course, the names have been changed. Here are some comments directly from course participants. Inaccurate grammar and spelling have been left as written:

Woman: "Miss P. - you are a wonderful woman. Thanks for listening to all of us women. Because of the course and YOU, I have devoted myself to laying down the old story and writing a new script that begins with right now. I actually did not know what real peace was until I took this course. Gaining freedom from emotional bondage is not easy. I was one of the people who had a hard time accepting responsibility for my own emotional health. I kept thinking if things would change, if other people would change then I would be alright. It never occurred to me that I was suffering from the years of abuse and rejection I had gone through. I really thought that was all behind me. You made me see that even though it was no longer happening to me physically, it was all recorded in my emotions and in my mind. That I was still feeling the effect of it."

Man: "She takes time out to explain and actually listen to us. I, for one, am very happy I took the class. Because if I would have never met my teacher, as I call her, I wouldn't of known that I have feelings and am man enough to cry for someone I really care about. And it's OK. Thank you for showing me another way to look at life!!"

Woman: "Coming into this group I didn't know much of a direction of handling my situations, understanding any one of my problems on a deeper level. My one way thinking always caused me to crash in everything in my life. In my eyes it was a one way path racing through in high speeds, and I didn't care who got hurt or about myself in the process. My inner core was the problem that I learned through the self help work. I just couldn't let go of my past and those who hurt me. I kept a pattern to repeat itself and couldn't stop it unless I truly excepted it. I had to pick up from start, take my wonder child through life again to be able to grow up healthy for once. Had to put in the work to find me. When I felt my triggers, my feelings I had to learn to stop, pause and reflect on a better energy level to gain focus on what I'm fighting for. I learned it's me. I am fighting TO SAVE ME!"

Man: "I have learned about an entire new part of me that is the made up me that gets in the way. As I was growing up I never realized that I was putting up barriers when I thought that I was setting standards to fit in or be like everyone else. These false standards include from being Mr. tough guy, the stereo typical, to acting the part of perfection as if nothing wrong has ever happened. This falsehood has created a fictitious place within where nonsense ran amuck. I always wondered why I never knew the reason and that's because I never looked in the right place, within. There I was looking more at what I do other then who I am. The scared child from the home where my drunk father would beat my mother. Although he never hit us, my sister, he may as well have because witnessing violence of that kind is knowing that can just as well be me. The sub personalities that I've learned about that I've built are extensive but thanks to the Houses of Healing (Mrs. P) I am aware of them now and know the healing will begin. Thanks for everything Mrs. P."

Most come in with low self-esteem, addiction issues and no true pride - just facades built up to protect fragile, scared inner-children who have learned how to protect themselves. The majority have never known anyone who really cared about them. They come from backgrounds of substance abuse, physical and sexual abuse, and abandonment. The women are often more damaged but may have already done some inner work and know how to share with another person. Men tend to be loners and need to learn how to open up. They tend to experience the most dramatic changes and biggest breakthroughs during the program. Whereas women jump eagerly into the program, men feel great resistance until they get positive feedback from other men. That is why the course is structured so that people can join during the first four weeks. It is not unusual to see the men's class start out with 10-12 men and swell to 20-25 by week four.

The *Houses of Healing* program speaks directly to the situations and feelings that these people struggle with in a way that they have never considered before. It offers emotional support and constructive ways to deal with the emotional issues that most of them developed in childhood. Beyond that, the program shows them that they can create a different kind of life by taking responsibility for their own thoughts and actions. There is a powerful emphasis on the need for forgiveness, for self and others, and direction is offered on how to achieve this.

Pris lets them know early on that they are much more than the sum total of any mistakes they have made. Since they have been told all of their lives that these mistakes show what losers they are, this is a new framework for them. Her credibility and trust factor are enhanced dramatically as she briefly shares some of her own imperfections through the stories of her childhood issues plus those she has had with her own children in going through the learning process. She makes it clear that issues are bound to come up in everyone's life. These, however, can be undone with recognition of the causes and in the knowledge that it is never too late to make amends.

The Reward

Following your Bliss, doing what you find you were born to do, ALWAYS brings the reward of feeling a life fulfilled, but it shows up in different forms. With her therapy practice, being witness to lasting changes in others' lives was a wonderful, but rare, experience. With *Houses of Healing*, she almost always gets to see noticeable, personal, positive changes over the thirteen weeks. Always a sucker for the underdog, Pris sees inmates as forgotten people — an underserved group. They come to her as people who have made mistakes and see them entirely as "their fault." She teaches them how to deal effectively with the underlying causes and how addictions can push them to act on raw emotion, negating their ability to reason or consider consequences. She has come to treasure watching the "aha" moments in people's processes and seeing a group of strangers bond into a family. The participants come hesitantly and guardedly to the first week of class with all of their defenses firmly in place. Then she is thrilled to watch the light bulbs go on as they look back on their childhoods and see the reasons behind their life choices, addictions, and the personalities in which they have become "stuck." She is as joyful as they are when they learn that they can face their mistakes, separate what they've <u>done</u> from who they <u>really</u> are, and take responsibility for their future. When people really get it that their <u>action</u> may be unforgivable but that they can forgive themselves, the person who committed the act, then they can leave the past in the past and create a very different future. When Pris witnesses that, she feels like the luckiest person on earth, because she was able to be the one to help initiate this change in their life.

The hardest weeks for Pris are the first and thirteenth. That first week, the inmates have no trust in their eyes. She finds that painful even though she knows that will soon disappear, replaced by, not only trust but, respect and even love. It's that love that develops that makes the last class so hard as it may be the last time she ever sees them. By that last class, they are asking the meaningful questions: "What changes have I made?" "Who am I now?" "How do I see things now?" "How do I see other people now?" This is when they see how all the pieces fit together that lead to their imprisonment and how they can build a new path leading to a very different destination. That's what brings Ms. P. back class after class.

People ask her how she can do all this work without getting paid. They have no idea that for her it is truly a privilege.

Postscript

Things haven't been perfect in this process. Pris's beloved husband Bob was diagnosed with cancer in 2003. She abandoned the prison work for 2 1/2 years to be by his side as he went through his final years of life. Following that, she went to work with Hurricane Rita victims. Upon her return, she discovered that her best friend was also a cancer victim. She felt like she was reliving the experience with Bob as she tended to her friend's needs up to her death a year and a half later.

In 2008, Pris returned to do more classes at the men's prison, but not to the women's prison. In 2011, Pris was thrilled to introduce Robin Casarjian, creator of the course, who had come to do a talk at a prison chaplain's conference. The chaplain of the women's prison convinced Pris that she should start doing courses there again, which she did for the next three years.

In 2014, Pris once again bowed out of the women's prison program. Changes in administration policies created difficulties with the women in "Max" being released to attend the classes on a regular basis, and the consistency of the program material was, therefore, compromised. Leaving the house early in the morning and driving 45 minutes to the facility only to find most or all of the women absent left her feeling powerless and frustrated. Even though it is the most satisfying work she's ever done and the women loved it, Pris felt her time there was at an end. Fortunately, through networking, she was able to find two women, with fresh enthusiasm, who were eager to be trained to take over the classes. They are teaching on "grounds," and positive changes in policy are helping to make their classes full and rewarding.

Since the men's prison is a minimum security facility, the flow of inmates is somewhat less stringent, so Pris happily continues those classes to this day.

The success of these classes underlines how much more effective our prison system would be if they truly were run as places for healing rather than punishment. The recidivism rate is said to be about 14% for inmates who complete this course versus 65% for the general prison population based on a 1994 Bureau of Justice report. That is the difference that dedicated people like Ms. P. can make.

EPILOGUE

If you've gotten this far, then you have read, and I hope enjoyed, the stories of thirteen people. This range included men and women, young and old, black and white, and spanned four continents (that is, assuming that Costa Rica is considered part of South America. I have never been sure which continent includes Central America and I'm very happy that my college degree didn't hinge on that).

More important, you have been exposed to people whose passion revolved around their vocation, relationship, geography, and/or volunteer work. You have met people who knew what their passion was from a very early age and others who didn't discover it until later in life. You have seen how the form of bliss may morph and even change dramatically as an individual moves along their life path. You have seen thirteen very different faces of bliss. My hope is that it is now obvious that it can take any shape.

There are two things that these thirteen people have in common. The first is their openness to recognize the right fit for them when it reveals itself. The second is their courage to do what it takes to follow that path. My wish for you is that you are also blessed with this vision and courage. Everything else will follow.